Unlock Your Creativity with Macrame Jewelry Making

Advanced Techniques and Captivating Designs Book

Andrew W Silva

THIS BOOK BELONGS TO
The Library of

....

....

Thank you for Purchasing my book and taking the time to read it from front to back. I am always grateful when a reader chooses my work and I hope you enjoyed it!

With the vast selection available online, I am touched that you chose to be purchasing my work and take valuable time out of your life to read it. My hope is that you feel you made the right decision.

I very much would like to know what you thought of the book. Please take the time to write an honest and informative review on Amazon.com. Your experience and opinions will be of great benefit to me and those readers looking to make an informed choice.

With much thanks.

Table of Contents

SUMMARY

The Art of Macrame Jewelry Making: The Art of Macrame Jewelry Making is a comprehensive guide that delves into the intricate world of creating stunning jewelry pieces using the ancient technique of macrame. This book is a must-have for anyone interested in exploring their creativity and learning the art of macrame jewelry making.

The book begins with an introduction to the history and origins of macrame, providing readers with a deeper understanding of this unique craft. It then moves on to explain the basic tools and materials needed to get started, ensuring that even beginners can dive right into the world of macrame jewelry making.

The Art of Macrame Jewelry Making covers a wide range of techniques, from the basic knots to more advanced patterns and designs. Each technique is explained in detail, with step-by-step instructions and accompanying illustrations to ensure clarity and ease of understanding. The book also includes helpful tips and tricks to help readers master each technique and create their own unique jewelry pieces.

One of the highlights of this book is the wide variety of projects it offers. From bracelets and necklaces to earrings and anklets, there is something for everyone. Each project is accompanied by detailed instructions, including a list of materials needed and a step-by-step guide to creating the piece. The book also provides inspiration for readers to customize and personalize their creations, encouraging them to experiment with different colors, beads, and embellishments.

In addition to the practical aspects of macrame jewelry making, this book also explores the artistic side of the craft. It delves into the principles of design, color theory, and composition, helping readers create visually appealing and aesthetically pleasing jewelry pieces. The book also includes tips on how to market and sell macrame jewelry, making it a valuable resource for those looking to turn their passion into a business.

The Art of Macrame Jewelry Making is not just a guide, but a source of inspiration and creativity. It encourages readers to explore their own unique style and experiment with different techniques and materials. Whether you are a beginner or an experienced macrame artist, this book is sure to enhance your skills and take your jewelry making to the next level.

Overall, The Art of Macrame Jewelry Making is a comprehensive and detailed guide that covers all aspects of macrame jewelry making. With its clear instructions, inspiring projects, and valuable tips, this book is a valuable resource for anyone interested in this ancient craft. Whether you are a hobbyist or a professional, this book is sure to become an essential part of your macrame library.

Introduction to Macrame and Its History: Macrame is a versatile and intricate form of textile art that involves knotting cords together to create various decorative and functional items. It has a rich history that dates back thousands of years and has been practiced by different cultures around the world.

The origins of macrame can be traced back to ancient times, with evidence of its existence found in the decorative knotting techniques used by the ancient Egyptians and Assyrians. These early civilizations used macrame to create intricate patterns and designs on clothing, accessories, and even furniture.

However, it was during the 13th century that macrame gained widespread popularity in Europe. Sailors, who spent long periods at sea, used macrame to pass the time and create useful items such as hammocks, belts, and bags. The sailors would often trade their macrame creations with locals during their travels, spreading the art form to different parts of the world.

During the Victorian era in the 19th century, macrame experienced a resurgence in popularity as a decorative art form. It was used to create elaborate curtains, tablecloths, and even jewelry. Macrame was considered a symbol of wealth and status, with intricate designs and patterns showcasing the skill and creativity of the artisans.

In the 1960s and 1970s, macrame became closely associated with the hippie and bohemian movements. The art form was embraced as a way to express individuality and creativity, with macrame plant hangers, wall hangings, and jewelry becoming popular among the counterculture.

Today, macrame continues to be a popular craft and art form. It has evolved to incorporate modern designs and materials, with artists experimenting with different types of cords, beads, and embellishments. Macrame workshops and classes are widely available, allowing people of all ages and skill levels to learn and create their own macrame pieces.

The appeal of macrame lies in its versatility and the endless possibilities it offers. From simple keychains and bracelets to intricate wall hangings and wedding backdrops, macrame can be adapted to suit any style or purpose. Its tactile nature and the rhythmic process of knotting can also be therapeutic and meditative, providing a sense of calm and relaxation.

In conclusion, macrame is a timeless art form with a fascinating history. From its ancient origins to its modern-day resurgence, macrame has captivated people with its intricate designs and creative possibilities.

Essential Macrame Jewelry Tools and Materials: When it comes to creating stunning macrame jewelry pieces, having the right tools and materials is essential. Macrame is a technique that involves knotting cords together to create intricate patterns and designs. Whether you are a beginner or an experienced macrame artist, having the right tools and materials can make a significant difference in the quality and outcome of your jewelry pieces.

One of the most important tools you will need for macrame jewelry making is a set of sharp scissors. These scissors will be used to cut the cords to the desired length and to trim any excess material. It is crucial to have sharp scissors to ensure clean and precise cuts, as this will contribute to the overall neatness and professionalism of your finished jewelry pieces.

Another essential tool for macrame jewelry making is a set of tapestry needles. These needles are used to weave the cords through the knots and create intricate patterns. Tapestry needles come in various sizes, so it is important to have a range of sizes to accommodate different cord thicknesses and designs. These needles should have a large eye to easily thread the cords through.

In addition to scissors and tapestry needles, a macrame board or mat is also a valuable tool to have. This board or mat provides a stable surface for knotting and weaving the cords. It helps to keep the cords in place and prevents them from tangling or slipping. A macrame board or mat also provides a clear grid pattern that can be helpful for creating symmetrical designs and ensuring accuracy in your knotting.

When it comes to materials, the most common choice for macrame jewelry is waxed cotton cord. This cord is durable, easy to work with, and comes in a wide range of colors and thicknesses. Waxed cotton cord has a slight stiffness to it, which makes it easier to manipulate and create tight knots. It also has a natural sheen that adds a beautiful finish to your jewelry pieces.

In addition to waxed cotton cord, you may also want to consider using beads and charms to add a unique touch to your macrame jewelry. Beads can be threaded onto the cords and incorporated into the knotting patterns, while charms can be attached to the finished jewelry pieces using jump rings. Beads and charms come in various shapes, sizes, and materials, allowing you to customize your jewelry pieces to suit your personal style and preferences.

Lastly, having a good quality jewelry clasp or closure is essential for finishing off your macrame jewelry pieces.

Knot Terminology and Basic Techniques of Macrame Jewelry Making: Knot terminology and basic techniques are essential aspects of macrame jewelry making. Macrame is a versatile and ancient art form that involves creating intricate patterns and designs by tying knots with various types of cords or threads. Whether you are a beginner or an experienced crafter, understanding the terminology and mastering the basic techniques will help you create stunning macrame jewelry pieces.

One of the fundamental aspects of macrame jewelry making is knot terminology. Familiarizing yourself with the different types of knots will enable you to follow patterns and instructions more easily. Some common knots used in macrame include the square knot, half hitch knot, lark's head knot, and the spiral knot. Each knot has its own unique characteristics and uses, and learning how to execute them correctly is crucial for creating beautiful macrame jewelry.

The square knot is one of the most commonly used knots in macrame. It is formed by crossing two cords and tying them in a specific sequence. This knot creates a flat, symmetrical pattern and is often used to create the body of a macrame jewelry piece. The half hitch knot, on the other hand, is a simple knot that is used to secure cords in place. It is formed by looping one cord around another and pulling it through the loop. This knot is commonly used to create fringe or tassels in macrame jewelry.

Another important knot in macrame jewelry making is the lark's head knot. This knot is used to attach cords to a base or to create loops for attaching clasps or pendants. It is formed by folding a cord in half, placing the folded end over the base cord, and pulling the loose ends through the loop. The lark's head knot is versatile and can be used in various ways to add decorative elements to your macrame jewelry.

The spiral knot is a more advanced knot that creates a spiral or twisted effect in macrame jewelry. It is formed by crossing two cords and wrapping one cord around the other in a spiral motion. This knot requires precision and practice to achieve the desired effect. The spiral knot is often used to create intricate patterns and textures in macrame jewelry, adding depth and visual interest to the design.

In addition to knot terminology, mastering the basic techniques of macrame jewelry making is essential for creating high-quality pieces. These techniques include measuring and cutting cords, securing cords to a work surface, and maintaining tension while tying knots.

Exploring Complex Knots for Jewelry Making: Exploring Complex Knots for Jewelry Making is a comprehensive guide that delves into the intricate world of knotting techniques specifically designed for jewelry making. This guide is perfect for both beginners and experienced jewelry makers who are looking to expand their repertoire and create stunning and unique pieces.

The book starts off by providing a thorough introduction to the art of knotting, explaining its history and significance in jewelry making. It then progresses to cover the basic knots that every jewelry maker should be familiar with, such as the square knot, the lark's head knot, and the half hitch knot. These foundational knots are explained in detail, with step-by-step instructions and accompanying illustrations to ensure a clear understanding.

Once the basics are covered, the book delves into more complex knots that are specifically tailored for jewelry making. These knots include the double coin knot, the Chinese button knot, and the Josephine knot, among others. Each knot is explained in depth, with detailed instructions on how to create them and suggestions on how they can be incorporated into various jewelry designs.

What sets this guide apart from others is its emphasis on creativity and experimentation. The author encourages readers to not only learn the knots but also to explore different variations and combinations to create their own unique designs. The book provides inspiration through a gallery of stunning jewelry pieces that showcase the versatility and beauty of these complex knots.

In addition to knotting techniques, the guide also covers other essential aspects of jewelry making, such as choosing the right materials, tools, and findings. It offers practical tips on how to select the appropriate cords and threads for different knotting projects, as well as advice on how to properly finish and secure the knots to ensure durability.

Furthermore, the book includes troubleshooting sections that address common challenges and mistakes that jewelry makers may encounter while working with complex knots. These sections provide helpful solutions and tips to overcome these obstacles, ensuring that readers can confidently tackle any knotting project.

Whether you are a novice jewelry maker or an experienced artisan, Exploring Complex Knots for Jewelry Making is a valuable resource that will inspire and guide you in creating intricate and stunning jewelry pieces. With its detailed instructions, creative ideas, and troubleshooting tips, this guide is a must-have for anyone looking to elevate their knotting skills and take their jewelry making to the next level.

Adding Intricate Patterns and Textures of Macrame Jewelry Making: Macrame jewelry making is an art form that involves creating intricate patterns and textures using various knotting techniques. This ancient craft has gained popularity in recent years due to its unique and stylish designs. By adding intricate patterns and textures to macrame jewelry, artisans can elevate their creations to a whole new level of beauty and complexity.

One of the key elements that sets macrame jewelry apart from other forms of jewelry making is the use of knots. These knots are not only functional in securing the various components of the jewelry together, but they also serve as decorative elements. By incorporating different types of knots, such as square knots, half-hitch knots, and lark's head knots, artisans can create stunning patterns and textures that add depth and visual interest to their pieces.

In addition to knots, macrame jewelry makers often incorporate other techniques to enhance the overall design. For example, they may use beads, gemstones, or charms to add a touch of sparkle and color to their creations. These embellishments can be strategically placed within the macrame patterns to create focal points or to highlight certain areas of the jewelry.

Furthermore, artisans can experiment with different types of cords and threads to achieve different textures in their macrame jewelry. Thicker cords can create a chunkier and more substantial look, while thinner threads can result in a delicate and intricate appearance. By combining different textures, such as smooth and rough cords, artisans can create a visually interesting contrast that adds depth and dimension to their pieces.

The possibilities for creating intricate patterns and textures in macrame jewelry are endless. Artisans can draw inspiration from various sources, such as nature, geometric shapes, or cultural motifs, to create unique and personalized designs. They can also experiment with different color combinations to further enhance the visual appeal of their creations.

Adding intricate patterns and textures to macrame jewelry not only elevates the aesthetic value of the pieces but also showcases the skill and creativity of the artisan. Each knot, bead, and thread is carefully chosen and meticulously crafted to create a one-of-a-kind piece of wearable art. Whether it's a statement necklace, a delicate bracelet, or a pair of earrings, macrame jewelry with intricate patterns and textures is sure to make a bold and stylish statement.

Combining Knots for Unique Designs in Macrame Jewelry Making: Macrame jewelry making is a popular craft that involves creating intricate designs using knots. One way to make your macrame jewelry stand out is by combining different knots to create unique and eye-catching designs.

There are numerous types of knots that can be used in macrame jewelry making, each with its own distinct look and texture. By combining these knots, you can create endless possibilities for your designs. For example, you can combine the square knot, which is a basic knot used in macrame, with the lark's head knot, which is commonly used to attach cords to a base. This combination can create a beautiful and intricate pattern that adds depth and dimension to your jewelry.

Another way to combine knots is by using different types of cords or materials. For instance, you can use a thicker cord for the base of your design and a thinner cord for the knots. This contrast in texture and thickness can create a visually appealing and unique look.

Furthermore, you can experiment with different color combinations to make your macrame jewelry even more distinctive. By using cords in different colors, you can create patterns and designs that are truly one-of-a-kind. For example, you can alternate between two different colored cords when creating a knot, or you can use multiple colors in a single knot to create a gradient effect.

In addition to combining knots, cords, and colors, you can also incorporate other elements into your macrame jewelry designs. For instance, you can add beads, charms, or pendants to your knots to create a focal point or add a touch of personalization. These additional elements can enhance the overall look of your jewelry and make it even more unique.

When combining knots for unique designs in macrame jewelry making, it is important to have a clear vision of the final design you want to achieve. Planning your design beforehand and experimenting with different knot combinations can help you create a truly unique piece of jewelry.

In conclusion, combining knots for unique designs in macrame jewelry making allows you to unleash your creativity and create stunning pieces that stand out. By experimenting with different knot combinations, cords, colors, and incorporating additional elements, you can create jewelry that is truly one-of-a-kind. So, let your imagination run wild and start creating your own unique macrame jewelry designs today!

Principles of Jewelry Design in Macrame Jewelry Making

Macrame jewelry making is a popular craft that involves creating intricate and beautiful pieces using various knotting techniques. While the process of macrame jewelry making may seem simple, there are several principles of jewelry design that can greatly enhance the final result. These principles include balance, proportion, color, texture, and focal point.

Balance is an important principle in macrame jewelry design as it ensures that the piece is visually appealing and harmonious. Balance can be achieved through the distribution of elements such as knots, beads, and charms throughout the design. Symmetrical balance involves creating a mirror image on both sides of the piece, while asymmetrical balance involves creating a sense of equilibrium through the careful placement of elements.

Proportion is another key principle in macrame jewelry design. It involves the relationship between the size and scale of different elements within the piece. Proportion can be used to create a sense of harmony and unity. For example, using larger beads or charms as focal points and smaller beads or knots as supporting elements can create a visually pleasing balance.

Color is an important aspect of macrame jewelry design as it can evoke different emotions and set the overall tone of the piece. The choice of colors should be carefully considered to create a cohesive and visually appealing design. Complementary colors, which are opposite each other on the color wheel, can create a vibrant and eye-catching effect. Analogous colors, which are adjacent to each other on the color wheel, can create a more harmonious and soothing effect.

Texture is another principle that can greatly enhance the design of macrame jewelry. Different types of cords, beads, and knots can create a variety of textures, adding depth and interest to the piece. Combining smooth and rough textures can create a visually dynamic design. Additionally, incorporating different materials such as leather, metal, or gemstones can further enhance the texture of the piece.

Lastly, the focal point is an important principle in macrame jewelry design. The focal point is the element that draws the viewer's attention and serves as the main point of interest in the piece. It can be achieved through the use of a larger bead, a unique knotting technique, or a special charm. The focal point should be strategically placed to create a sense of balance and visual interest.

In conclusion, understanding and applying the principles of jewelry design in macrame jewelry making can greatly enhance the final result.

Choosing the Right Colors and Materials of Macrame Jewelry Making: When it comes to macrame jewelry making, choosing the right colors and materials is crucial in creating stunning and unique pieces. The colors and materials you select can greatly impact the overall look and feel of your jewelry, making it essential to carefully consider your choices.

Firstly, let's discuss the importance of color selection. The colors you choose for your macrame jewelry can convey different emotions and moods. For example, vibrant and bold colors such as red, orange, and yellow can create a sense of energy and excitement. On the other hand, soft and pastel colors like light blue, pink, and lavender can evoke a feeling of calmness and tranquility. It's important to think about the message you want your jewelry to convey and select colors accordingly.

Additionally, consider the color combinations you use in your macrame jewelry. Complementary colors, which are opposite each other on the color wheel, can create a striking contrast and make your jewelry stand out. For example, pairing blue and orange or purple and yellow can create a visually appealing and eye-catching effect. Analogous colors, which are next to each other on the color wheel, can create a harmonious and cohesive look. For instance, combining shades of blue and green or red and orange can create a sense of unity in your jewelry design.

Moving on to materials, the choice of materials can greatly impact the overall quality and durability of your macrame jewelry. One popular material for macrame jewelry making is cotton cord. Cotton cord is soft, lightweight, and easy to work with, making it ideal for creating intricate macrame designs. It also comes in a wide range of colors, allowing you to easily find the perfect shade for your jewelry.

Another material commonly used in macrame jewelry making is nylon cord. Nylon cord is known for its strength and durability, making it suitable for creating long-lasting jewelry pieces. It is also available in various thicknesses, allowing you to choose the right cord size for your desired design.

In addition to cords, beads and gemstones can also be incorporated into macrame jewelry. Beads can add a touch of elegance and sophistication to your designs, while gemstones can bring a natural and earthy element. When selecting beads and gemstones, consider their color, shape, and size to ensure they complement your macrame design.

Creating Balance and Proportion in Your Designs of Macrame Jewelry Making: Creating balance and proportion in your designs of macrame jewelry making is essential to achieve visually pleasing and harmonious pieces. Macrame jewelry making involves the intricate art of knotting various cords and threads together to create beautiful and unique accessories. By understanding and implementing principles of balance and proportion, you can elevate your macrame jewelry designs to a whole new level.

Balance refers to the distribution of visual weight in a design. It is important to create a sense of equilibrium in your macrame jewelry pieces, ensuring that no single element overpowers the others. There are two types of balance that you can incorporate into your designs: symmetrical and asymmetrical balance.

Symmetrical balance involves creating a mirror image on either side of a central point. This can be achieved by using the same knots, patterns, and materials on both sides of your macrame jewelry piece. Symmetrical balance creates a sense of stability and formality, making it suitable for more traditional and classic designs.

On the other hand, asymmetrical balance involves distributing visual weight unevenly across a design. This can be achieved by using different knots, patterns, and materials on each side of your macrame jewelry piece. Asymmetrical balance creates a sense of movement and dynamism, making it suitable for more contemporary and modern designs.

Proportion, on the other hand, refers to the size and scale of different elements in a design. It is important to ensure that the proportions of your macrame jewelry pieces are visually pleasing and harmonious. One way to achieve proportion is by considering the size of the wearer and the intended purpose of the jewelry piece.

For example, if you are creating a macrame bracelet, you would want to ensure that the size of the knots and beads used are proportionate to the size of the wearer's wrist. Similarly, if you are creating a macrame necklace, you would want to ensure that the length and size of the pendant or focal point are proportionate to the wearer's neckline and body shape.

In addition to balance and proportion, it is also important to consider the color scheme and texture of your macrame jewelry designs. The colors you choose should complement each other and create a cohesive and harmonious look. Similarly, the textures of the cords and threads used should add depth and interest to your designs.

Overall, creating balance and proportion in your designs of macrame jewelry making is a crucial aspect of achieving visually pleasing and harmonious pieces.

Crafting Stunning Macrame Bracelets of Macrame Jewelry Making: Crafting stunning macrame bracelets is a popular form of macrame jewelry making. Macrame is a technique that involves knotting cords together to create intricate and beautiful designs. Macrame bracelets are a great way to showcase this art form and create unique and personalized accessories.

To begin crafting macrame bracelets, you will need a few essential materials. These include macrame cord, which can be made from various materials such as cotton, hemp, or nylon. You will also need scissors to cut the cord, a ruler or measuring tape to ensure accurate lengths, and a closure mechanism such as a button or a clasp.

Once you have gathered your materials, you can start by measuring and cutting the cord to the desired length. This will depend on the size of your wrist and the design you want to create. It's important to measure accurately to ensure a comfortable fit.

Next, you can start knotting the cord to create the bracelet. There are various macrame knots that you can use, such as the square knot, the spiral knot, or the half-hitch knot. Each knot creates a different pattern and texture, so you can experiment with different combinations to achieve the desired look.

As you knot the cord, you can also incorporate beads or charms to add extra flair to your macrame bracelet. These can be threaded onto the cord before you start knotting or added in between knots. Beads and charms can be made from various materials such as glass, wood, or metal, allowing you to customize your bracelet to your liking.

Once you have completed the knotting and added any desired embellishments, you can finish off the bracelet by attaching a closure mechanism. This can be a button that is sewn onto one end of the bracelet, or a clasp that is attached using jump rings. The closure mechanism should be secure enough to hold the bracelet in place while also being easy to fasten and unfasten.

Crafting stunning macrame bracelets requires patience and attention to detail. It is a process that allows for creativity and self-expression, as you can experiment with different knotting techniques, colors, and materials. The end result is a unique and personalized piece of jewelry that can be worn with pride or given as a thoughtful gift.

In conclusion, macrame bracelets are a beautiful and intricate form of macrame jewelry making. By using various knots, incorporating beads or charms, and adding a closure mechanism, you can create stunning and personalized bracelets.

Mastering the Art of Micro Macrame: Mastering the Art of Micro Macrame is a comprehensive guide that delves into the intricate world of micro macrame, providing readers with a wealth of knowledge and techniques to create stunning and intricate macrame designs on a smaller scale. This book is perfect for both beginners who are just starting out in the world of macrame, as well as experienced macrame artists looking to expand their skills and explore new techniques.

The book begins with an introduction to the history and origins of macrame, providing readers with a deeper understanding of the art form and its cultural significance. It then moves on to cover the essential tools and materials needed for micro macrame, ensuring that readers are well-equipped to embark on their macrame journey.

One of the standout features of this book is its detailed step-by-step instructions for a wide range of micro macrame projects. From delicate bracelets and necklaces to intricate wall hangings and plant hangers, readers will find a plethora of inspiring projects to choose from. Each project is accompanied by clear and concise instructions, accompanied by detailed photographs and diagrams, making it easy for readers to follow along and create their own stunning macrame pieces.

In addition to the project tutorials, Mastering the Art of Micro Macrame also includes chapters dedicated to teaching readers various macrame techniques. From basic knots and braids to more advanced techniques such as adding beads and incorporating color, readers will learn how to master each technique and apply them to their own unique macrame designs.

Furthermore, the book also provides valuable tips and tricks for troubleshooting common macrame challenges, ensuring that readers are able to overcome any obstacles they may encounter during their macrame journey. Whether it's dealing with tangled cords or achieving the perfect tension, readers will find practical solutions to help them create flawless macrame pieces.

Mastering the Art of Micro Macrame is not just a practical guide, but also a source of inspiration. The book features stunning photographs of finished macrame pieces, showcasing the endless possibilities and creative potential of micro macrame. Readers will be inspired to experiment with different colors, textures, and patterns, and to push the boundaries of their own creativity.

Overall, Mastering the Art of Micro Macrame is a must-have resource for anyone interested in macrame. With its comprehensive coverage of techniques, detailed project tutorials, and inspiring photographs, this book is sure to become a go-to reference for macrame enthusiasts of all skill levels. Whether you're a beginner looking to learn the basics or an experienced artist seeking to refine your

Projects At A Glance

Rambling Cadence Bracelet

Sweet Sugar Plum Bracelet

Weathered Branch Bracelet

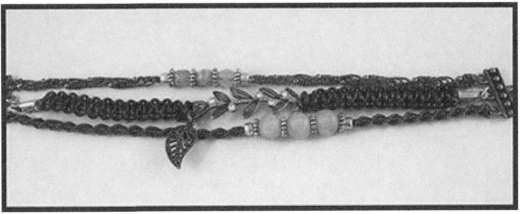

Glacial Storm Bracelet

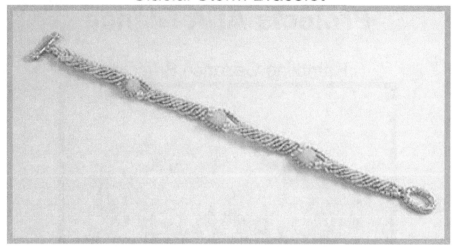

Mountain Ice Bracelet

Lunar Eclipse Arm Cuff

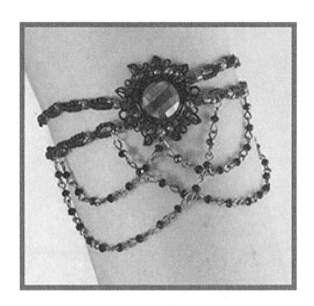

Red Letter Day Earrings

Raspberry Frost Donut Bead Necklace

Eye of the Storm Pendant

Wildwood Necklace

Introduction

In the beginning, there were knots. From bridge building to horse hitching to sailing and lace making, knots have been an important part of history. Micro macramé is an updated twist on an antiquated practice.

In an era of instant gratification, there is something empowering about taking a piece of cord or leather, and creating a beautiful design from it. However, learning on your own can be difficult and my desire is to write my patterns as clearly as possible so that you can pick up the basics, have success in the beginning and see satisfying results quickly.

When I first began to explore micro-macrame, I showed my mom a picture of a necklace. She took one look and so "Oh, so you don't wear it; it's an art piece". That has stuck with me over the years and has inspired me to keep my designs wearable.

When looking at various jewelry designs, I found that most items were tightly woven, or highly elaborate and time consuming. My preference is towards more open designs, so I try to keep my jewelry light. Whether striving for a casual or extravagant piece, I lean toward a flowing, lacework look.

There are no fancy, expensive tools required for this hobby and relatively little space is needed, although it is a good idea to have adequate lighting.

Time to get creative! Choose your colors and let's begin. With easy to follow step by step instructions, you CAN do this, it's "knot" that hard to learn!

General Supplies

The Essential Project Board

There are several different kinds of padded board designs available on the internet. Some are made of foam and others of cork. There are also some available for purchase in bead stores that are not foam, but instead have a scalloped edge that allows you to wedge your cord in between the scallops, provided your cords are long enough to reach the edge of the board.

I prefer to use thick foam which gives me the ability to push my straight pin all the way in, using the head to hold the cord tightly when necessary. A feature I used often when I was first learning. I also often pin horizontally across a cord to give it some tension without piercing the cord itself.

To make my board, I started with a leftover piece of foam that was lying around. (Ok, it was lying around at my mom's house, but it was in the attic, so it's fair game, right?) As you can see I made a rough cut that is actually a bit larger than my clip board. This is about 12in x 13in. Where the top clip will be, I cut out a slope.

Next I added about 4 inches to each side and cut out my fabric. Choose wisely here. On my first try I used a very light, soft pink fabric that was a flannel type of material. When I worked on a project though, especially picking up beads to string onto the cords, I was forever having little bits of fluff on my fingers and in my way. Cotton is a better choice. Cover the foam with your fabric. Turn to the back and safety pin it in place. I like to be able to take the cover off to wash it (there may be a coffee spill in the future) or just change it out if it doesn't work (like the aforementioned pink stuff).

Turn to the front and fit onto your clipboard.
I keep straight pins in the top corners of my board, which I use to pin cords, hold the fastenings (closures), or keep a focal bead for later use my current project.

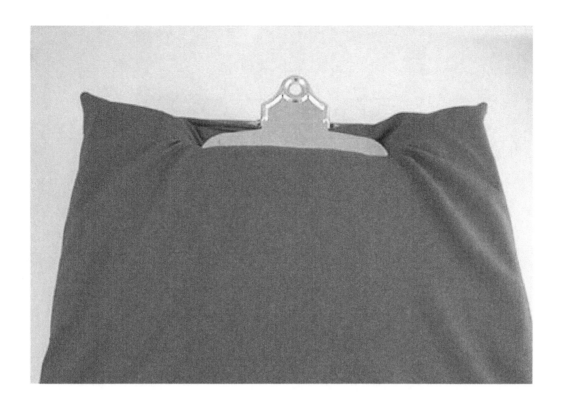

Tools

Reaming tools

The right beads can really complement your project. What fun it is finding the perfect shape and color, then rushing home to work it into your creation – and what disappointment if you then spend hours wrestling with the tiny bead opening which is stubbornly refusing to go on to your cord.

So what is the solution? A simple set of bead reamers. I most often use the smallest one, but I have had occasion to reach for the next size up also. My reamers are for use on glass, ceramic, pearl and stone beads. This tool can literally smooth the way with tricky beads.

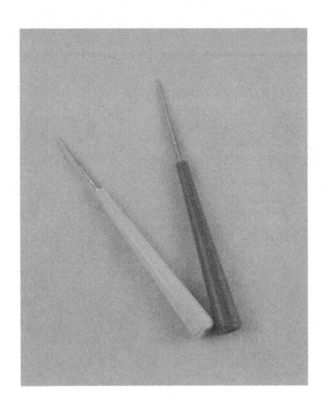

Beading tools
It is a good idea to have some basic beading tools on hand. Several patterns have jump rings or ribbon clasp closures which would benefit from the use of (shown from left to right) needle nose pliers, round nose pliers, a crimp tool and wire cutters. You will also need a pair of small, sharp scissors. And I do mean sharp; if they are dull they will fray the cord when you cut it.

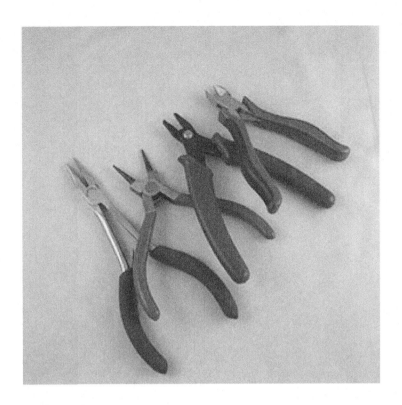

Glue

Often in micro-macramé, your only loose ends are at the end of the project when you tie it all off. In my experience, this is your weakest link. So why not strengthen it as best as you can? Many people use nail polish; I prefer glue. One type if glue you can use is E6000. It works well on leather and many jewelry makers prefer to use it.

Another good choice is Beacon 527 multi-purpose glue. It dries clear, though shiny. Usually I leave it to dry well (often overnight) then trim my cords and apply a second coat.

Note: Some crafters use a singeing tool to fuse the ends of nylon cords, melting them together. This leaves a bit of black residue, so use this technique only on dark cords, or where it won't show like behind a focal bead or button.

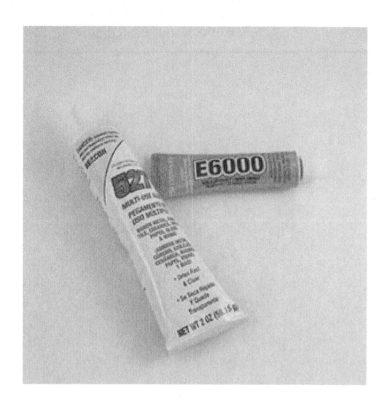

Pins

Straight pins are significant in micro-macramé design work. Some people prefer T-pins. Either way, a long shank is more comfortable to work with. Pins are vital when it comes to holding cords in place, and useful for teasing out a mistake without unraveling your cord.

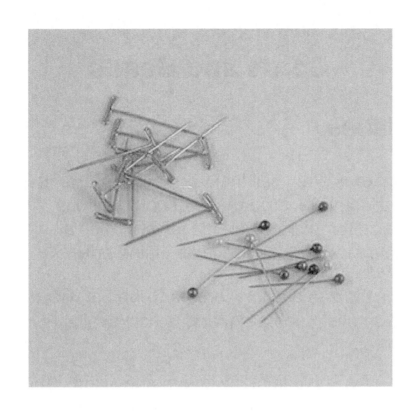

Cords and Beads

Cord Varieties

C-Lon - My patterns often call for C-Lon Bead Cord. It is a 3 ply nylon cord available in a large range of color options. This cord is the standard size for micro macramé jewelry. It is also available in smaller diameters. Currently available online only.

S-Lon – This is the same nylon cord as C-lon but with different color names, and a smaller spool size, and is now available in some brick and mortar stores.

Leather Cord – Available in many colors and sizes. Some are flat strips, others are round. You can buy leather, suede and faux leather as well. Leather resists knotting and can break, so it is generally used as an accent or only with less intricate knots like an overhand knot or a square knot.

Waxed Linen – As the name implies, this is a linen cord that was been lightly coated in wax. It comes in 3, 4 or 5 ply and is said to be colorfast. The wax layer prevents fraying, but does add a small amount of bulk to the cord, so small diameter beads will not thread onto it.

Bead Types

Metal –Non-precious metals which offer a less expensive alternative to silver and gold.

Crystal – It is the refraction created by many cuts on a glass surface that gives crystals their fancy shine.

Glass – This category is where you will find flamework and lampwork beads.   Versatile and affordable, glass bead are an excellent choice for novice beaders.

Semiprecious or gemstone – These beads are a popular choice as they offer a large variety of options. The list is extensive, so here are a just a few: agate, amber, garnet, jade, malachite and onyx.

Clay - These beads can be made of ceramic clay, which is fired in a kiln and glazed, or made of porcelain which generally involves a potter's wheel, a kiln, and hand painting. There is also polymer clay which is not technically a clay at all, but a plastic. This material is an oven- baked clay that can be used at home to make your own unique beads and is very versatile.

Other - There are also beads made from shell, such as mother of pearl, tiger shell, abalone, and conch shells. You may also come across wooden beads which come from the bark, roots or branches of many types of trees. Some wooden beads are carved and have been popular for generations.

Basic Knots

Lark's Head Knot

The Lark's head knot is great for attaching cords to key rings, jump rings, donut beads or spacer beads. You can also use it to attach cords onto a watch face to create a band.

Fold a cord in half. Take the loop and fold it over whatever you are attaching it to, from front to back as shown.

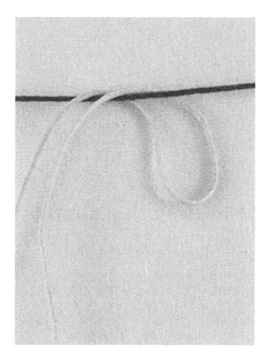

Take the two cords that are loose end cords and feed them through the loop.

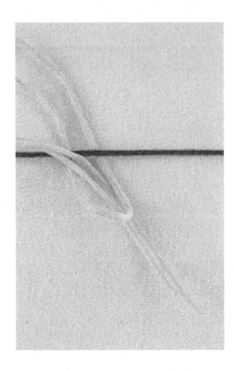

Now pull gently and evenly on the ends to tighten it up.

Overhand Knot

This knot is often used at the end of loose cords to keep them from fraying. It is sometimes used at the beginning of a pattern when attaching a cord to other cord.

Make a loop, push one end through, and pull cords to tighten.

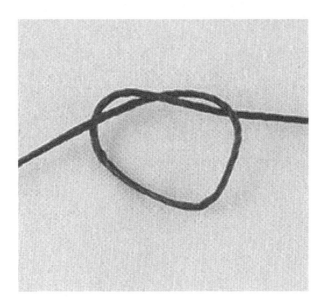

Square Knot

This is one of the most popular knots in micro-macrame. You can work the knot beginning with either the right cord or the left. I usually begin with the left cord. It is most often worked using two outer cords and two or more inner or holding cords.

Place the left cord over the holding cords. Then place the right most cord over top of the tail of the left cord.

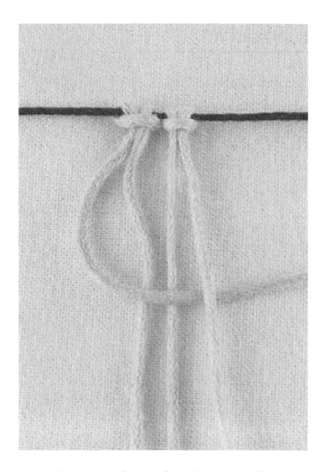

Take the right cord and move it under the holding cords, then out over the left cord.

Gently pull the left and right cords to tighten up the first half of the square knot. Now place the right cord over the holding cords. Move the left cord over top of it the tail of the right cord.

Run the left cord underneath the holding cords and out over the right cord.

Here is the finished Square Knot:

Here are several in a row, which is called a sennit:

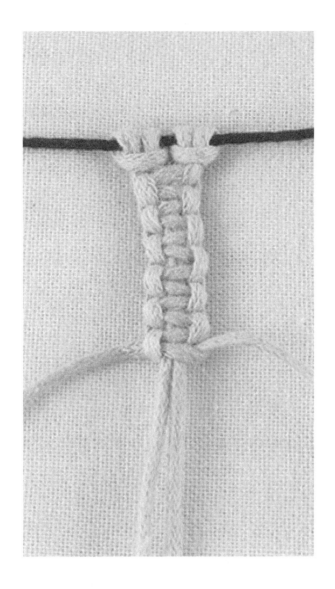

Spiral Knot

A half knot is the first half of a square knot. If you tie several in a row, they naturally begin to twist and you get a spiral effect. You can create a left or a right spiral.

To create a left spiral, place the left cord over the holding cords then move the right cord over top of the left.

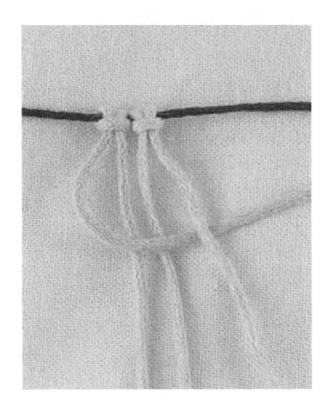

Slide the right cord under the holding cords then out and over the left cord.

Tighten it up. Then take the left cord again and put it over the holding cords, moving the right cord over top of the tail if the left cord.

Thread the right cord under the holding cords, then out and over the left cord.

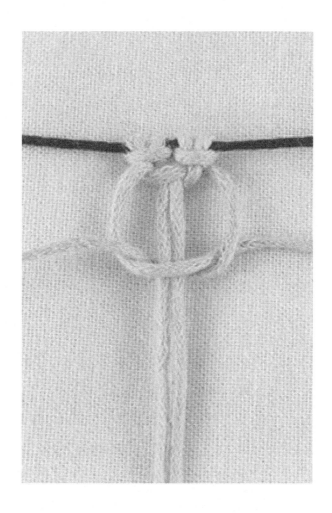

Repeat this a few more times and you will see the spiral forming.

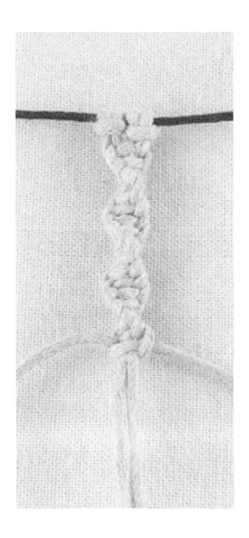

To create a right spiral you would need to tie knots from only the right side. Then your spiral would twist the opposite way and look like this:

Alternating Lark's Head Chain with Vertical Lark's Head Knot Variation

This knot may look harder than it is. Once you get going it is pretty easy and fun. Just think over-under-over, then under-over-under.

Take the right cord and lay it over the center cords (this can be done with only 1 holding cord if desired), then under the center two cords back to the right, making sure to pass over the shaft of the right cord.

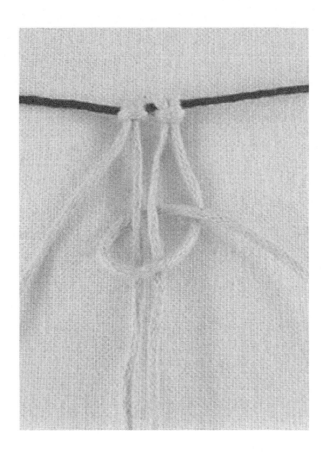

You will want to tighten that up, but for now I will show you the next half of the knot. Take the right cord and move it under the center two cords then over the center two back to the right, making sure to pass under the shaft of the right cord.

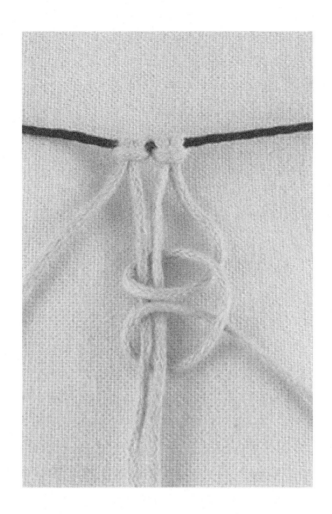

Here is what it looks like cinched up:

Repeat previous with the left cord (still around the center two cords). Work over, under, over and draw it up tight, then work under, over, under.

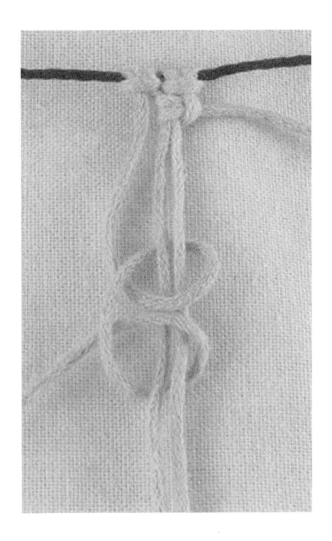

Here is the second knot tightened up.

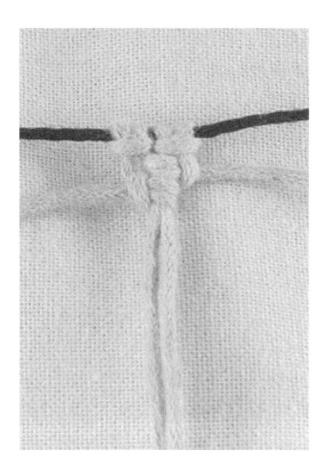

You can alternate sides to create a chain of knots.

Variation: If you tie knots from only one side, it is a Vertical Lark's Head Knot and looks like this:

Half Hitch Knot

This is a very simple knot that is often used in repetition.

Take your working cord and place it over top of your holding cord. Pass it under the holding cord and back over the shaft of the working cord itself.

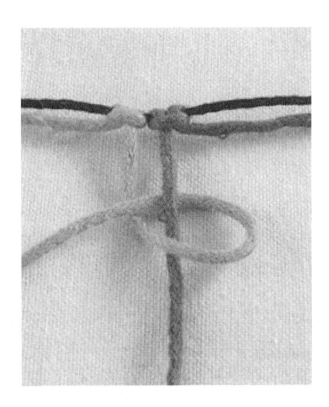

Gently pull the working cord until it tightens up at the top of the holding cord.

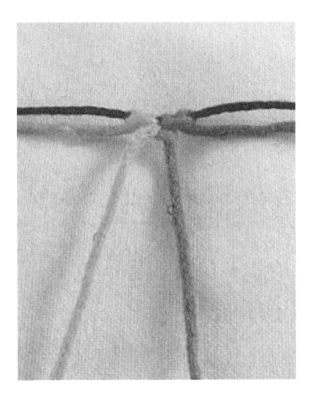

Diagonal Double Half Hitch Knot

This knot is a little tricky, but with just a bit of practice you will be able to get a feel for the right amount of tension you need to help you master it. You can work this knot from either side. We will start on the left.

Take the left cord and lay it diagonally over top of all the other cords. This is the holding cord onto which the knots will be tied.

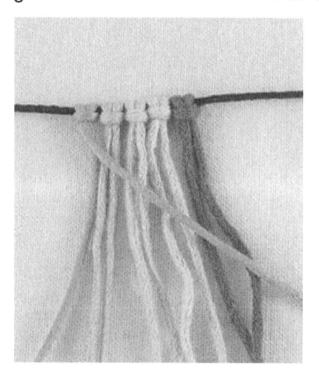

Take the cord on the left and, from underneath, wrap it up and around the holding cord. Be sure the tail end of the wrapping cord passes over the cord shaft. Gently snug the knot up to the top of the holding cord.

Repeat a second time with the same cord to complete the double half hitch.

Repeat with the remaining cords. This is a completed diagonal double half hitch from left to right:

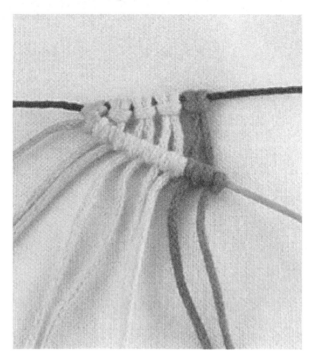

Now we will work a diagonal double half-hitch from right to left. I will just continue on with the arrangement I have going. Instructions will be the same if you are starting a new project.

Take the cord from the right and lay it diagonally over all the other cords to the left. This is now your holding cord. Working with the adjacent cord, wrap it up around the holding cord, making sure the tail end crosses over its shaft.

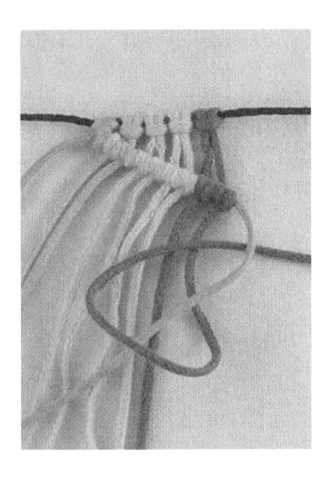

Snug it up and repeat a second time to finish the knot.

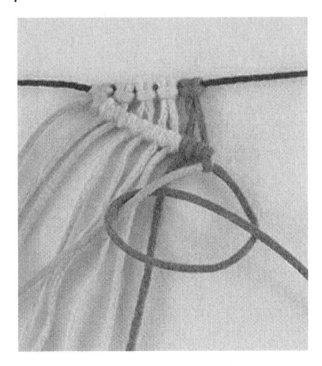

Repeat with the remaining cords. This is a row of Diagonal Double Half Hitch Knots from left to right, and then from right to left.

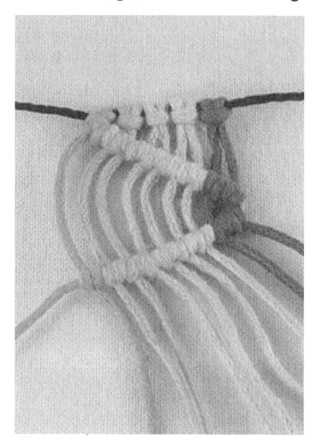

Reverse Half Hitch Knot Variation

This half hitch knot changes direction after each knot. When tied from one side then the other, the ridge you are creating stays to the back of the work.

Tie a half hitch knot from one side.

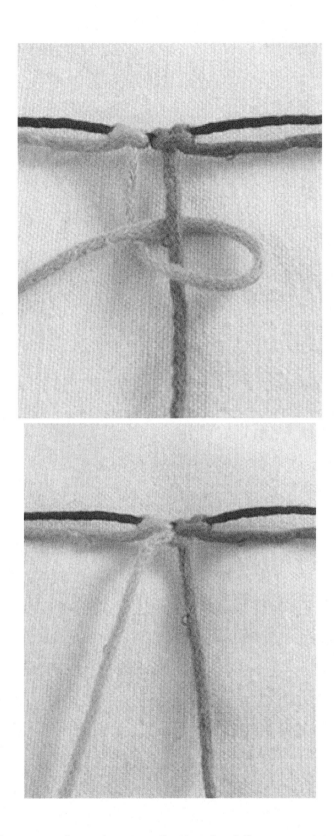

Move the working cord underneath the holding cord to the opposite side.

Tie a half hitch knot from this side.

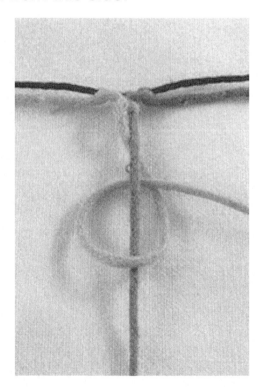

Continue to tie one HH knot, then pass the working cord underneath the HC to the opposite side and tie one HH knot.

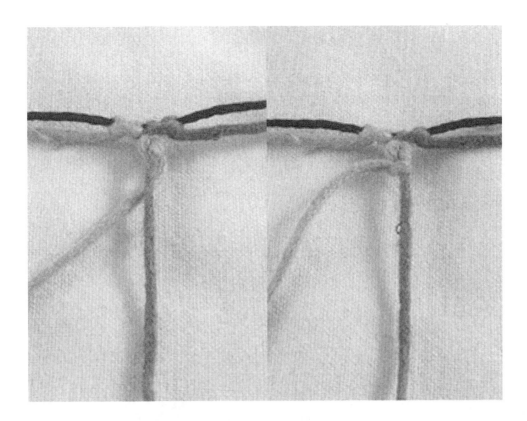

Several in a row will look like this:

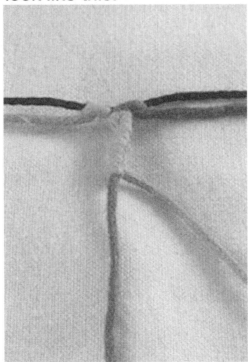

Horizontal Double Half Hitch Knot

This is a half hitch knot, tied twice onto a horizontal holding cord.

Place left cord to the left as the holding cord. To tie a half hitch knot onto it, bring the next cord up from below, around the holding cord and down, making sure to cross back over the shaft of the tying cord.

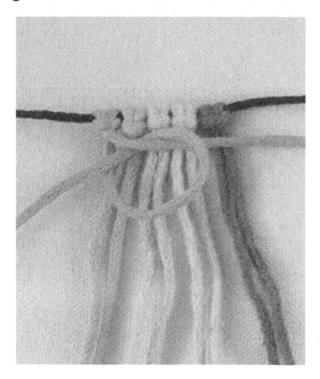

Repeat the half hitch once more with the same tying cord to create a double half hitch knot.

Tying a double half hitch knot onto the holding cord with the remaining cords it will look like this:

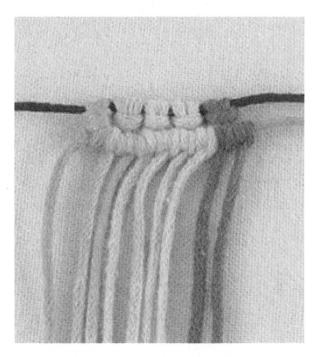

Vertical Double Half Hitch Knot

This knot will be tied so that the finished knot is vertical.

Move the knotting cord underneath the holding cord.

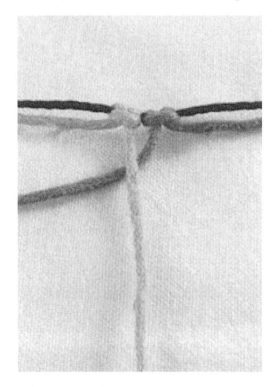

Tie a half hitch knot onto the holding cord.

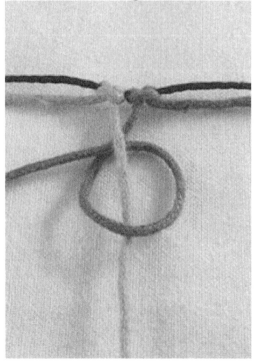

Tie a second half hitch knot to create a double half hitch.

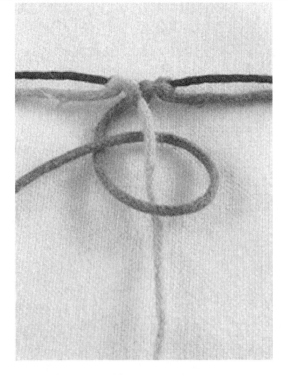

Notice that the finished knot is vertical on the holding cord.

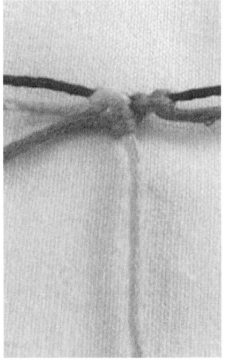

Tied from the opposite side:

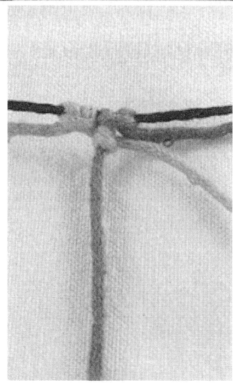

Rambling Cadence Bracelet

A double half hitch knot, and the humble square knot work in harmony to create this edgy bracelet. Made with Black C-Lon cord and black iridescent beads, this piece also incorporates a toggle clasp. The finished length is about 7 inches and it can be easily lengthened.

Supplies:
Black C-Lon cord, 3 cords, 7 ft each
8mm oval black iridescent beads, 10
Size 6 iridescent seed beads, 30
Size 8 black seed beads, 20
Silver toggle clasp set, 1
Glue

1. Take a cord and fold it in half. Attach to one end of the toggle clasp set using a Lark's Head knot. Repeat with the 2 remaining cords.

2. Tie a Square Knot (SK) with left 3 cords.

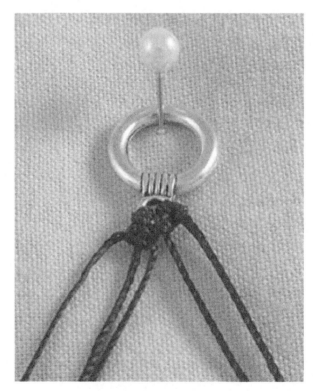

3. Find the 4th cord from the right and move it up and to the right as the Holding Cord (HC). Tie a Diagonal Double Half Hitch (DDHH) knot onto it with each of the next three cords, working from left to right.

4. Place the 3rd cord in from the right up and to the right as the HC. Tie a DDHH knot onto it with each of the next 2 cords, working from left to right.

5. Move the right cord down and to the left as the HC. Tie a DDHH knot onto it with each of the next 2 cords, working from right to left.

6. Place a size 6 seed bead onto the 4th cord from the right. Move the right cord down and in toward the center then tie a DDHH knots onto it with each of the next 3 cords, working from right to left.

7. Repeat steps 3-6 twice.

8. Place the two left cords together and thread on a size 8 seed bead, an 8mm oval bead, and another size 8 seed bead.

9. Place all cords together and use the left cord and the right cord to tie a SK.

10. Find the 4th cord from the left and move it up and to the left as the HC. Tie a DDHH knot onto it with each of the next 3 cords, working from right to left.

11. Place the 3rd cord in from the left to the left as the HC. Tie a DDHH knot onto it with each of the next 2 cords, working from right to left.

12. Move the left cord down and to the right as the HC. Tie a DDHH knot onto it with each of the next 2 cords, working from left to right.

13. Place a size 6 bead onto the 4th cord from the left. Move the left cord down and in toward center then tie a DDHH knots onto it with each of the next 3 cords, working from left to right.

14. Repeat steps 10-13 twice.

15. Place the two right cords together and thread on a size 8 seed
bead, an 8mm oval bead, and another size 8 seed bead. Repeat
step 9.

16. Repeat steps 3-15, four times, or until desired length. You can stop after step 9, or step 15 depending which fan shape you end with.

17. Tie 2 more SK around the 4 center cords.

18. Turn the piece so that the loose cords are at the top of your work surface, then flip the bracelet to the back side. Take the center 4 cords and place them through the unused part of the toggle clasp, then place the cords straight down. Tie a square knot with the outer 2 cords around all others. Glue the knot, then trim the excess cords (or trim cords, leaving a slight stub then singe with a singe tool - for best results use on dark cords only).

Sweet Sugar Plum Bracelet

This delightful design gives you the opportuntiy to weave a lattice section that is delicate enough to compliment the flower button focal bead. C-lon cord, various beads and a decorative silver clasp are all that is called for to complete this 7 ½ inch bracelet.

Supplies:
Eggplant C-Lon cord, 8 cords, 4 ft each
Lavender flower button with shank, about 1 inch, 1
4mm purple bicone beads, 8
Size 6 lavender seed beads, 12
Silver toggle closure set, 1
5mm silver jump rings, 2
Glue

1. Take one cord and fold it in half. Place it horizontally across you work surface. Take a second cord and fold it in half. Attach onto the horizontal cord using a Lark's Head Knot (LHK). Repeat with 6 more cords.

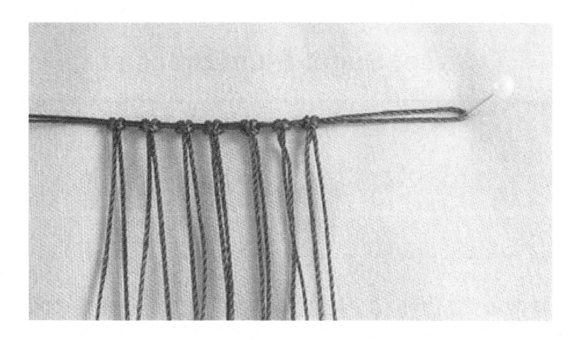

2. Place the ends of horizontal cord through the shank on the button, then through the beginning loop of same cord. Slowly tighten and move 8 cords to the top and 8 cords to the bottom. (The cords that went through the shank and loop are now on the bottom right).

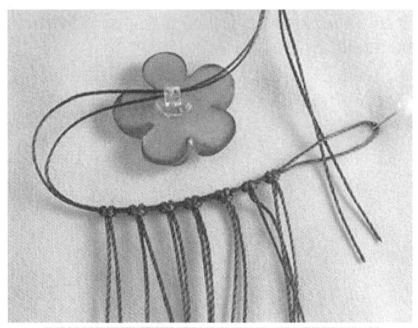

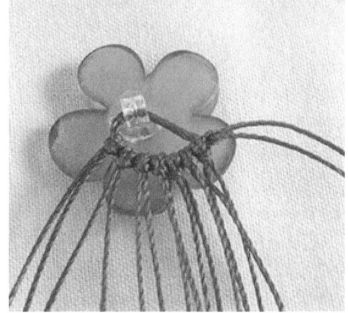

3. If your centerpiece has holes in it, pin it to your work surface. If not, you can tape the top cords down for this first part. For now we will still work from the back side (these knots will be hidden behind the button and it is a lot easier to tie this row from the back). Separate cords 4-4. Move the left cord to the right as the Holding Cord (HC) then tie a Diagonal Double Half Hitch (DDHH) knot onto it with each of the next 3 cords working from outside to inside. Move the right cord to left as the HC and tie a DDHH knot onto it with each

of the next 3 cords working from outside to inside. Now turn over to the front, and repeat 5 times.

4. Take a size 6 light purple seed bead and place the left and the right center cords through it, one from each side.

5. Separate cords 2-2-2-2. Working with the left 2 cords; use the right cord to tie a Reverse Half Hitch (RHH) knot onto the left cord. Begin from the right side, then move the cord under to the left side and repeat until you have 17 RHH knots.

6. Working with the right 2 cords; use the left cord to tie a RHH knot onto the right cord. Begin from the left side, then move the cord under to the right side and repeat until you have 17 RHH knots.

7. Take the inner 2 left cords and use the outer cord to tie 5 Vertical Lark's Head (VLH) knots onto inner cord. Repeat with the inner 2 right cords, using the outer cord to tie onto the inner cord.

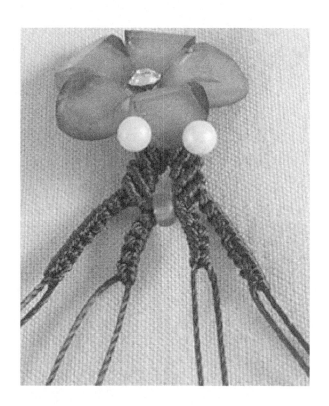

8. Repeat step 4.

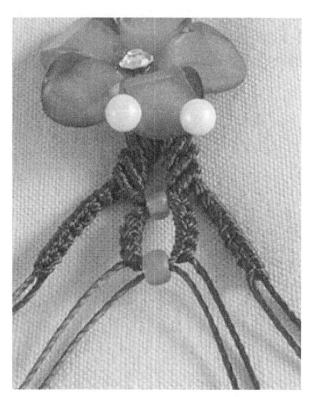

9. Move the 4th cord from the left to the left as the HC. Tie a DDHH knot onto it with each of the 3 left cords, working from inside to outside.

10. Move the 4th cord from the right to the right as the HC. Tie a DDHH knot onto it with each of the 3 right cords, working from inside to outside.

11.   Place a 4mm bicone bead onto each outer cord. Separate cords 4-4. Set aside left and right cord. Weave the center 6 cords. Begin with inner right cord and weave it to the left over the first cord, then under the second then over the third. With the next right cord weave to the left under, over, under. The third cord is woven the same way as the first one.

12.   Move the left cord to the right as the HC. Tie a DDHH knot onto it with each of the next 3 cords, working from outside to inside. Move the right cord to the left as the HC. Tie a DDHH knot onto it with each of the next 3 cords working from outside to inside.

13. Repeat step 4.

14. Repeat steps 5-7.

15. Repeat step 8-13.

16. Separate cords 2-2-2-2. Using the left 2 cords; use the right cord to tie a RHH knot onto the left cord. Begin from the right side, then move the cord under to the left side and repeat until you have 15 RHH knots. Using the right 2 cords; use the left cord to tie a RHH knot onto the right cord. Begin from the left side, then move the cord under to the right side and repeat until you have 15 RHH knots.

17. Repeat steps 7 & 8.

18. Separate cords 4-4. Move the outer left cord in to the center as the HC. Tie a DDHH knot onto it with each of the next 3 cords, working from outside to inside. Repeat once (or more if you want to lengthen it).

19. Move the outer right cord in to the center as the HC. Tie a DDHH knot onto it with each of the next 3 cords, working from outside to inside. Repeat once (or more if you want to lengthen it).

20.   Separate cords 3-2-3. Tie a SK with each set of 3 cords. Place all cords together and tie a SK with the outer cord on each side.

21.   Add a silver jump ring to each end of the toggle clasp set. Turn to the back side of the bracelet. Now rotate so that the loose cords are at the top of your board. Place the center 6 cords through the jump ring then back down toward you, laying them on top of the bracelet. Use the outer cord on each side to tie a square knot around the center cords (but not around the bracelet). Place a dab of glue on the square knot and let it dry. Trim excess cords.

22.   Repeat steps 3-21 for the opposite side of the bracelet. Here is the bracelet in another color scheme:

Weathered Branch Bracelet

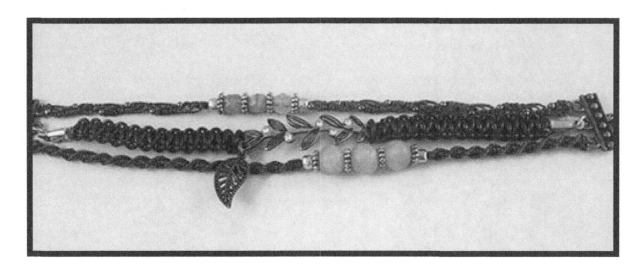

Leather cord brings a modern dimension to this fun, casual bracelet. Use this pattern to put some basic knots into practice. With 3 strands, a centerpiece and a charm, it also offers many versatile color options. The finished length is about 7 ½ inches.

Supplies:
Chocolate C-Lon cord, 4 cords, 5ft each
1mm round brown leather cord, two 1ft cords, two 3ft cords
8mm peach beads, 3
5mm peach beads, 3
6mm gold spacer beads, 8
Size 6 gold seed beads, 4
Size 11 gold seed beads, 16
About 4cm Branch centerpiece charm, 1
5mm fold over crimp ends gold, 2
15mm leaf charm, 1
4mm gold jump ring, 4 or 5
Gold 3 hole closure set, 1 (add jump rings and lobster clasp if necessary)
Glue

Center Section:

1. Take a 1ft leather cord and attach it to the opening of the center charm using a Lark's Head Knot (LHK).

2. Take a 3ft leather cord and center it horizontally under the first leather cord. Pin in place and use it to tie a Square Knot (SK) around the center cords. Continue tying SK for desired length (about 5 cm). Tip: Keep the center cords flat, and don't pull too tightly on the knottng cords or the leather will break.

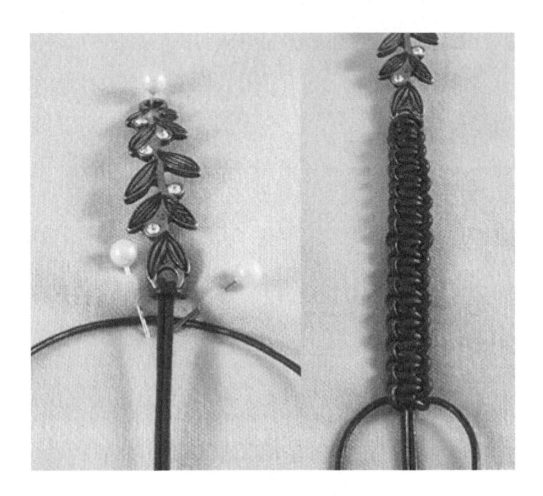

3. Repeat steps 1 & 2 on the opposite side of the centerpiece.

4. For both ends: glue the center 2 cords into a crimp end (be sure the flat side of the crimp end will be on the outside of the bracelet). Add in the outer 2 cords, glue, then carefully crimp shut. Trim the cords and attach a jump ring to the crimp end, then attach the jump ring to the center of the 3 hole closure.

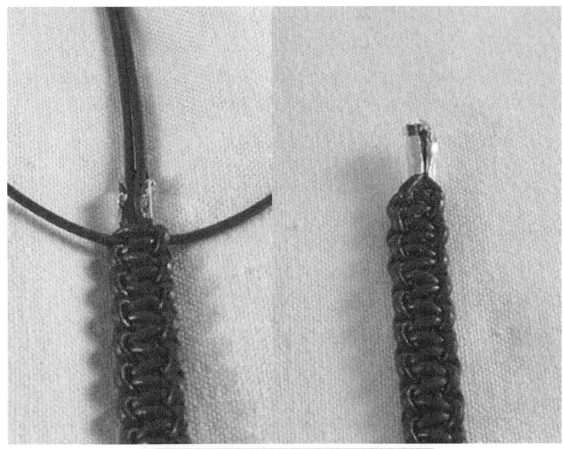

Left Section:
5. Take a 5ft Chocolate C-Lon cord and attach it to the left opening of 3 hole closure using a LHK. Repeat with another 5ft cord

6. Tie a Left Spiral Knot for a length of about 8 cm or until you reach roughly the center of the charm.

7. Thread all four cords through a size 6 gold seed bead. Next thread all cords through a gold spacer bead followed by a 7mm peach bead. Repeat a spacer bead and a 7mm bead twice. Follow with one more spacer bead and a size 6 gold seed bead.

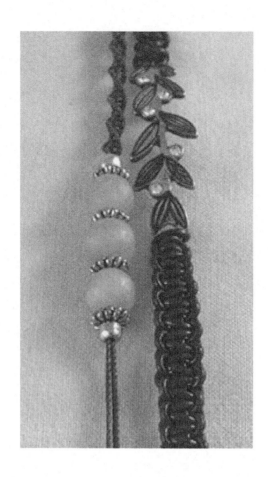

8. Move the short cords to the center as the holding cords. Use the outer cords to continue tying a Left Spiral Knot to match the length of the center leather section (about 4.5 cm).

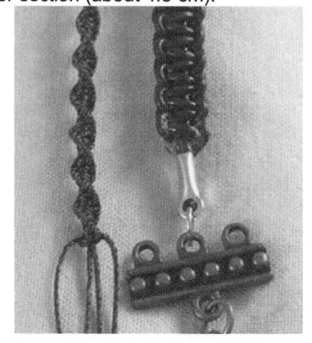

Right Section:

9. Take a 5ft Chocolate C-Lon cord and attach it to the right opening of 3 hole closure using a LHK. Repeat with another 5ft cord.

10.   Place a size 11 gold seed bead onto the left cord. Use the 3rd cord from the right to tie a Vertical Lark's Head (VLH) knot onto the beaded cord. Place this cord next to the beaded cord; they are now both holding cords.

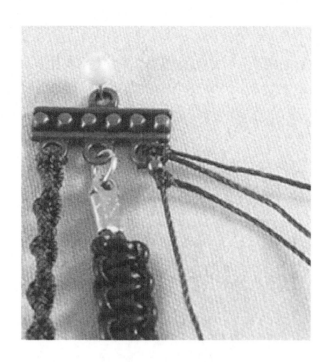

11.   Use the 2nd cord from the right to tie a VLH knot around both holding cords, then place this cord with the other 2 holding cords.

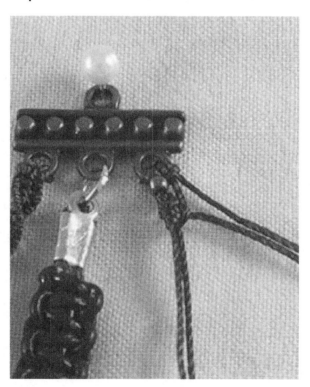

12.   Use the right cord to tie a VLH knot around all 3 holding cords.

13. Place a size 11 gold seed bead onto the right cord. Use the 3rd cord from the left to tie a VLH knot onto the beaded cord. Place this cord next to the beaded cord; they are now both holding cords.

14. Use the 2nd cord from the left to tie a VLH knot around both holding cords, then place this cord with the other 2 holding cords.

15. Use the left cord to tie a VLH knot around all 3 holding cords.

16.   Repeat steps 10-15 twice.

17.   Thread all four cords through a size 6 gold seed bead. Next thread all cords through a gold spacer bead followed by a 5mm peach bead. Repeat a spacer bead and a 5mm bead twice. Follow with one more spacer bead and a size 6 gold seed bead.

18. Repeat steps 10-15 five times.

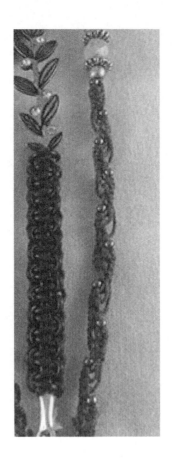

19.   Turn to the back side of the bracelet. With the left 4 cords, thread the center 2 cords through the left opening of the 3 hole closure, from underneath to the top. Bring the center 2 cords down toward you, laying them on top of the bracelet. Use the outer cord on each side to tie a square knot around the center cords (but not around the bracelet). Place a dab of glue on the last knot and let it dry. Trim excess cords. Repeat with the right 4 cords. Place a jump ring on one end of the 3 hole closure, and a jump ring and a lobster clasp on the other.

20. Attach the leaf charm to a jump ring (if necessary) and place the jump ring through the first opening on the center charm.

Glacial Storm Bracelet

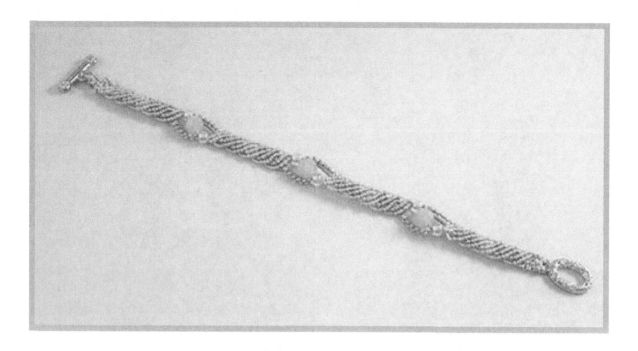

Using two colors of C-Lon cord, this sleek design offers a fun way to play with half hitch knots. Here we use mostly diagonal double half hitch knots, but also in use are vertical and horizontal double half hitch knots. If you want to adjust the 6 ¾" length of this bracelet you can either add more square knots at the very end (that option is written into the pattern) or you can change out the toggle closure for an adjustable length closure.

Supplies:
Silver C-Lon cords, 2 cords, 7 ½ ft
Ice Blue C-Lon cord, 1 cord 7 ½ ft
Silver toggle closure set, 1
Ice blue 6mm beads, 3
Ice blue size 6 seed beads, 6
Glue

Take a Silver C-Lon cord and fold it in half to find the center. Attach it to one end of the toggle closure using a Lark's Head knot. Repeat with an Ice Blue cord, placing it to the right of the Silver cord. Repeat with the other Silver cord, placing it to the right of the blue cord.

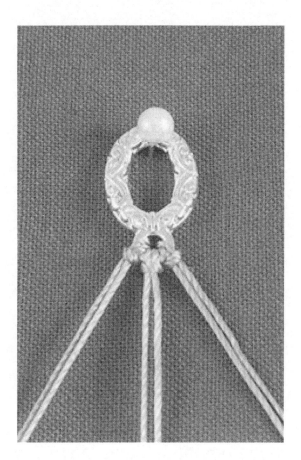

1. Separate cords 3-3. Tie one square knot with the left 3 cords. Tie two Square Knots (SK) with the right 3 cords.

2. Take the 2nd cord in from the left and move it to the right as the Holding Cord (HC). Tie a Diagonal Double Half Hitch (DDHH) knot onto it with each of the next 4 cords, working from left to right.

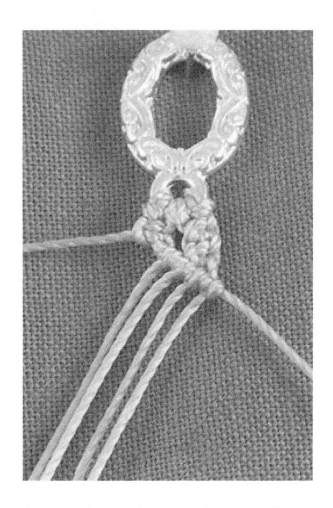

3. Take the left cord and move it to the right as the HC. Tie a DDHH knot onto it with each of the next 4 cords, working from left to right.

4. Use the 2nd cord from the left as the HC. With the 3rd cord in from the left, tie a Vertical Double Half Hitch (VDHH) knot onto the HC.

5. Move the 3rd cord from the left to the right as the HC. Tie a Horizontal Double Half Hitch (HDHH) knot onto it with the 4th cord, and then the 5th cord from the left. This creates an L shape.

6. Move the same HC to the right and use the right cord to tie a DDHH knot onto it.

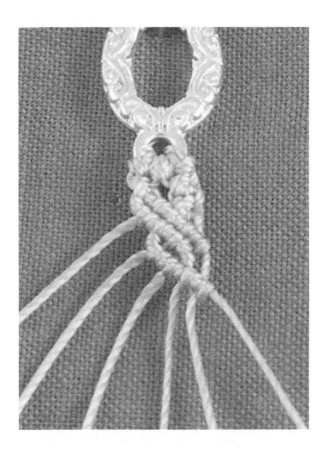

7. Take the left cord and move it to the right as the HC. Leaving a slight space (enough to match the space on the right cord), tie a DDHH knot onto it with each of the next 4 cords, working from left to right.

8. Repeat steps 2-7 twice.

9. Place the right 3 cords through a size 6 seed bead. Find the right cord and use it to tie 6 Vertical Lark's Head (VLH) knots onto the 2nd cord from the right.

10.   Use the left cord to tie 6 VLH knots around the 2nd and 3rd cord in from the left. Place a 6mm blue bead onto the 3rd cord in from the right, then thread a size 6 seed bead onto the left 4 cords.

11.   Repeat steps 2-7, three times.

12.   Repeat steps 9-11, twice.

13.   Separate cords 3-3. Tie two square knots with the left 3 cords.
Tie one SK with the right 3 cords.

14. Set aside each outer cord and tie 2 SK's with the center 4 cords. (To lengthen tie more square knots here).

15. Now turn so that the loose cords are at the top of your work surface, then flip the bracelet to the back side. Thread the toggle closure onto the center 2 cords, then place the cords straight down on top of the bracelet. Tie a square knot with the outer 2 cords around all others. Glue all end knots then trim the excess cords.

Mountain Ice Bracelet

C-Lon cord and seed beads merge with double half hitch knots to create this stunning button closure bracelet. Three larger beads create a center focal point in this jazzy yet casual piece. As written, this pattern creates a 7 inch bracelet and includes instructions to lengthen it if desired.

Supplies:
Steel C-lon cord, 5 cords 7ft
18mm silver shank button, 1
5mm blue-green beads, 3
Size 11 blue iridescent seed beads, 150
Glue

1. Place all cords together then find the center and tie a loose overhand knot. Pin onto your work surface as shown.

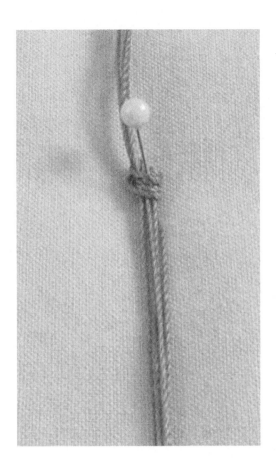

2. Use the outer cords to tie about 21 Square Knots (SK) below the overhand knot, then undo the overhand knot. Bend into a horseshoe shape placing all cords together. Tie a SK with the outer two cords. Test the size by placing the button through the button hole. It should fit snugly. Adjust knots as necessary.

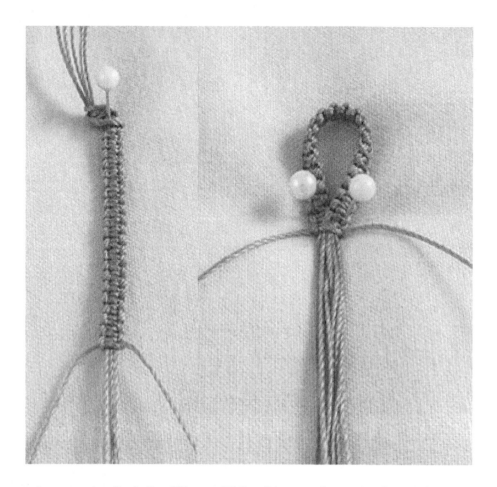

3. Separate cords 3-4-3. Tie a SK with each set of cords.

4. Separate cords 2-3-3-2 and tie a SK with each set of 3 cords.

5. Place a size 11 iridescent seed bead onto the left cord and move it to the right as the Holding Cord (HC). Tie a Diagonal Double Half Hitch (DDHH) knot onto it with each of the next 2 cords, working from left to right. Repeat four times.

6. Place a size 11 iridescent seed bead onto the right cord and move it to the left as the HC. Tie a DDHH knot onto it with each of the next 2 cords, working from right to left. Repeat four times.

7. Place a seed bead onto the 4th cord from left then move it to the right as the HC. Tie a DDHH knot onto it with the 5th cord from the left. Repeat once.

8. Place a seed bead onto the 4th cord from right then move it to the left as the HC. Tie a DDHH knot onto it with the 5th cord from the right. Repeat once.

9. Move the 5th cord from the right to the left as the HC. Tie a DDHH knot onto it with the 5th cord in from the left.

10.   Repeat steps 7-9.

11. Repeat steps 3 and 4.

12. Repeat steps 5-9.

13. Repeat steps 7-9.

14. Repeat steps 3 and 4.

15.   Repeat steps 5-11.

16.   Place the 3rd cord from the left to the right as the HC. Tie a DDHH knot onto it with each of the next 2 cords, working from outside to inside. Repeat once.

17.   Place the 3rd cord from the right to the left as the HC. Tie a DDHH knot onto it with each of the next 2 cords, working from outside to inside. Repeat once.

18. Place the center two cords through a 5mm bead, then move the center right cord to the right as the HC. Tie a DDHH knot onto it with each of the next 2 cords working from inside to outside. Use the 5th cord in from the right as the HC placed to the right. Tie a DDHH knot onto it with each of the next 2 cords working from inside to outside.

19. Move the center left cord to the left as the HC. Tie a DDHH knot onto it with each of the next 2 cords working from inside to outside. Use the 5th cord in from the left as the HC placed to the left. Tie a DDHH knot onto it with each of the next 2 cords working from inside to outside.

20. Place a seed bead onto the right cord. Take the 2nd cord in from the right and move it to the right as the HC. Tie a DDHH knot onto it with the right cord. Repeat 6 times.

21. Place a seed bead onto the left cord. Take the 2nd cord in from the left and move it to the left as the HC. Tie a DDHH knot onto it with the left cord. Repeat 6 times.

22.   Repeat steps 3 and 4.

23. Repeat steps 16-21.

24. Repeat steps 3 and 4.

25. Repeat steps 16-21.

26. Repeat steps 3 and 4.

27. Repeat steps 5-11 three times.

28. Repeat steps 3 and 4 (repeat this step to lengthen if desired).

29.   Place the center 4 cords together and use the 3rd cord in from the left and the 3rd cord in from the right to tie two SK around them.

30. Turn to the back side of the bracelet. Now rotate so that the loose cords are at the top of your board. Set aside the outer 2 left cords and outer 2 right cords. Thread the center 4 cords only through the button shank (leaving one left cord and one right cord to tie with). Place the center 4 cords down on top of the bracelet. Use the nearest single cord on each side to tie a SK around the center cords.

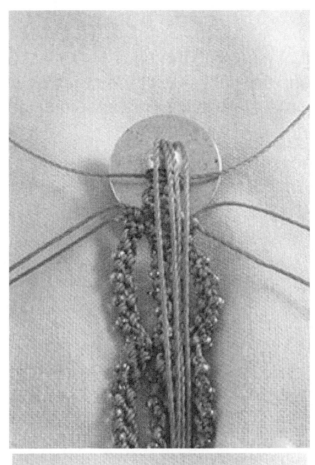

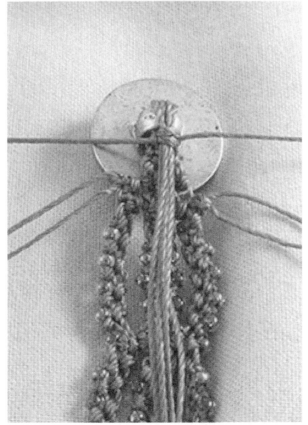

31. Place a bit of glue onto the back of the last SK, and the last knot on the left and the right side of the bracelet. Let dry, then trim the excess cords. Here is the finished piece in another color scheme.

Lunar Eclipse Arm Cuff

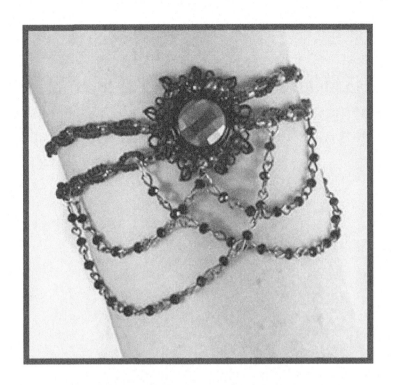

A striking blue centerpiece and a few shimmery gems ensure that this is not your traditional arm cuff! This eye-catching piece is made with Black C-Lon cord and an additional layer of texture is added with silver chain accents. It has an adjustable chain closure and the finished length is 9 inches, not including the closure (about 11 inches with it).

Supplies:
Black C-Lon cord, 8 cords, 5ft each
Size 6 light blue seed beads, 28
Size 8 silver seed beads, 28
Centerpiece that is about 1 inch in diameter, with openings to attach cords and chain, 1
4mm or 5mm silver jump rings, 9
3mm or 4mm silver crimp beads, 4
Silver adjustable closure set with a lobster clasp (or spring ring closure if you prefer), 1

Pliers

Crimp tool

Silver chain, about 16 inches (40cm). I purchased a beaded chain, but feel free to use a plain chain if you prefer

Glue

1. Take a cord and fold it in half. Attach it to the upper left side of your centerpiece using a Lark's Head Knot (LHK). Repeat with a second cord, then turn it so that the cords are straight down on your work surface.

2. Take a black cord and fold it in half. Attach it to the centerpiece on the right side of this knotted section using a Lark's Head Knot (LHK). Repeat with a second cord.

Left 4 cords:

3. Thread all 4 left cords through a size 6 light blue seed bead. Now place the left 2 cords through a size 8 silver seed bead. Note: You will want to keep track of the cords to reduce twisting. For example; the left cord needs to stay to the left all the way through.

4. Using the left cord, tie 3 Vertical Lark's Head (VLH) knots onto the second cord in from the left.

5. Using the right cord tie 5 VLH knots onto the second cord in from the right.

6. Place all 4 cords together and tie a Square Knot (SK).

7. Repeat steps 3-6 six times, or until desired length. Bear in mind that you want this piece to be a bit short of your arm circumference to allow room for an adjustable clasp, and that an armband needs to be tight to stay in place. You'll want to leave about 2 inches between the knotted ends.

Right 4 cords:

8. Place all 4 right cords through a size 6 light blue seed bead. Now place the right 2 cords through a size 8 silver seed bead.

9. Use the right cord to tie 3 VLH knots onto the second cord in from the right.

10. Use the left cord to tie 5 VLH knots onto the second cord in from the left.

11. Place all 4 cords together and tie a SK.

12. Repeat steps 8-11 six times, or until desired length.

Repeat steps 1 through 12 on the opposite side.

Check the fit before moving on. Adjust if necessary.

13.   Add a jump ring onto a lobster clasp (if necessary). Flip the arm cuff over so that the backside is facing up. Now turn it so that the loose cords are at the top of your work surface (either end, it doesn't matter at this point). Thread 4 cords through a large silver crimp

bead, then through the jump ring and back through the crimp bead. Do not crimp shut yet.

14. Attach the other 4 cords in the same way.

Before you crimp the crimp beads, make sure the knotted cords are all lying flat with no twists, and that the crimp bead is snug up against the last knot. Crimp the crimp beads and trim off excess cords.

15. Add a jump ring to an adjustable chain closure (if necessary). Turn the piece so that the remaining loose cords are at the top of your work surface (still with the backside facing up). Attach crimp beads as before, making sure the knotted cords are all lying flat. Crimp the crimp beads and trim off excess cords.

16.   To connect the chain:
Cut a 13.5cm length of chain and add a jump ring to both ends. Attach it around the lower set of VLH knots just to the right of the centerpiece.

Cut a 6.5cm length of chain and add a jump ring to both ends.
Attach it to the 3rd opening to the right of the centerpiece.

Take another 6.5cm length of chain and attach it onto the last jump ring on the other 6.5cm chain.

Cut a 13.5cm length of chain and add a jump ring to both ends.
Attach to the 5th opening to the right of the centerpiece.

Take the chain connected to the first loop and move it to the left, attaching it to the 5th opening out from the center.

Take the chain that is connected into the 3rd space to the right of the centerpiece and find the middle jump ring. Open the jump ring and connect it to the center of the centerpiece.

Find the jump ring on the end and attach it to the third opening to the left of the centerpiece.

Take the final chain and attach it to the first opening to the left of the centerpiece.

Red Letter Day Earrings

I really like the way these earrings turned out. The shape is lovely and keeping the beading to a minimum allows the rich color of the Red C-Lon cord to be the highlight. This pattern gives you a fast way to practice some Margaretenspitze (Margarete Lace) techniques. The finished length of the knotted piece is about 3cm.

Supplies:
Red C-Lon cord, 2 ft length, 8 cords (4 per earring)
4 or 5 mm gold jump ring, 2
Size 6 red seed beads, 2
Size 11 gold seed beads, 16
Size 11 red seed beads, 8
4mm gold spacer beads, 4
Gold ear wires, 2
Glue

1. Fold a cord in half and attach it to a gold jump ring using a Lark's Head Knot (LHK). Leave the opening of the jump ring accessible for

later use.

2. Take another cord and center it horizontally under the first set of cords. Attach it using an overhand knot. Repeat with 2 more cords.

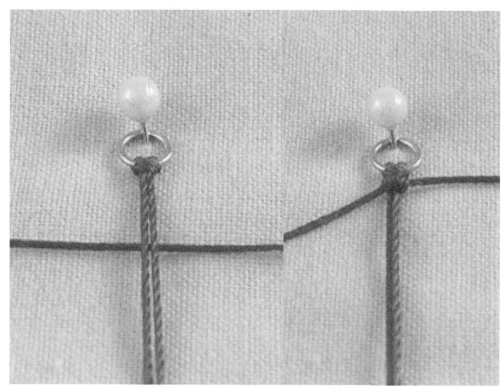

3. Separate the center 2 cords; the left cord to the left and the right cord to the right. Move the top left cord down and to the right as the

holding cord (HC). Tie a Diagonal Double Half Hitch (DDHH) knot
onto it with each of the next 3 cords working from outside to inside.

4. Move the top right cord down and to the left as the HC. Tie a
DDHH knot onto it with each of the next 3 cords, working from
outside to inside.

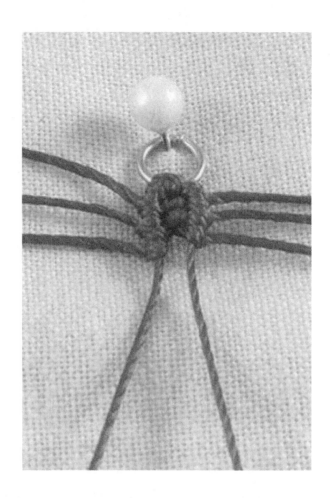

5. Move the center right cord over the center left cord. Tie a DDHH knot with the left cord onto the right.

6. Place a size 11 gold seed bead onto top left cord then move it down and in as the HC. Tie a DDHH knot onto it with each of the next 3 cords, working from outside to inside. Repeat once.

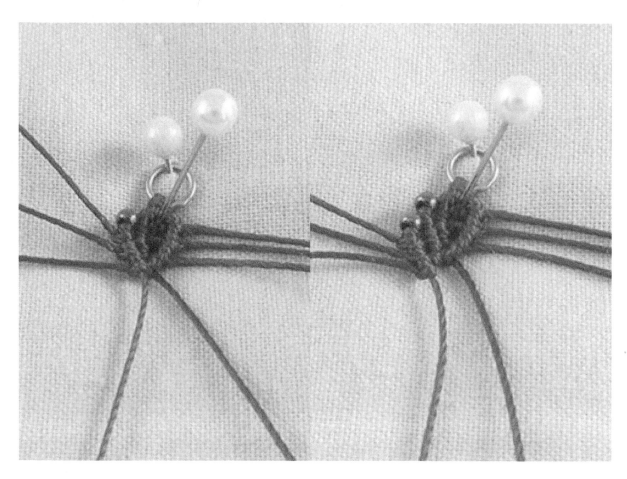

7. Place a size 11 gold seed bead onto top right cord then move it down and in as the HC. Tie a DDHH knot onto it with each of the next 3 cords, working from outside to inside. Repeat once.

8. Cords should now be separated 3-2-3.

9. Working with the left cords, move the 3rd cord from the left to the left as the HC. Tie a DDHH knot onto it with each of the next 2 cords, working from inside to outside.

10. Place a size 11 red seed bead onto 3rd cord from the left. Move the 2nd cord from the left to the left as the HC. Tie a DDHH knot onto it with left cord, then move this HC down and in to the right and tie a DDHH knot onto it with the same knotting cord.

11. Move the left cord to the right as the HC, then tie a DDHH knot onto it with each of the next 2 cords, working from outside to inside.

12. Repeat steps 9-11.

13. Working with the right cords, move the 3rd cord from the right to the right as the HC. Tie a DDHH knot onto it with each of the next 2 cords, working from inside to outside.

14. Place a size 11 red seed bead onto the 3rd cord from the right. Move the 2nd cord from the right to the right as the HC. Tie a DDHH knot onto it with the right cord, then move this HC down and in to the left and tie a DDHH knot onto it with the same knotting cord.

15. Move the right cord to the left as the HC, then tie a DDHH knot onto it with each of the next 2 cords, working from outside to inside.

16.   Repeat steps 13-15.

17. Find the center 2 cords and thread on a 4mm gold spacer bead, a size 6 red seed bead and another spacer bead.

18. Take the 4th cord from the right and move it to the left as the HC. Tie a DDHH knot onto it with the 4th cord from the left (the other center cord), then with the 3rd cord from the left.

19. Move the 4th cord from the right to the right as the HC. Tie a DDHH knot onto it with the 3rd cord from the right.

20. Working with the right 3 cords, place a size 11 gold seed bead onto the middle cord. Tie a SK with the outer cords. Set aside the right cord.

21. With the right 3 cords, place a size 11 gold seed bead onto the middle cord. Tie a SK with the outer cords.

22. Working with the left 3 cords, place a size 11 gold seed bead onto the middle cord. Tie a SK with the outer cords. Set aside the left cord.

23. With the left 3 cords, place a size 11 gold seed bead onto the middle cord. Tie a SK with the outer cords.

24. Find the center 4 cords and tie a SK.

25.   Turn the piece over and place some glue on the last knot of each cord. Let dry then trim excess cord (or you can trim the ends, then singe with a singeing tool, but this is usually only recommended for dark color cords). Open the jump ring and attach an ear wire.

26.   Repeat steps 1-25 for the second earring.

Raspberry Frost Donut Bead Necklace

This necklace has a knotting section above and below the donut bead that complement one another. The upper pattern can be continued on further if you like, or even used separately to create a lanyard. The finished length as written is about 15 inches (38cm).

Supplies:
Rose C-Lon cord, 4 cords cut to 5 ft each (for the upper section), 6 cords cut to 2 ft each (for the lower section)
3cm Donut bead
4mm raspberry beads, 4

Size 10 pink seed beads, 4
Beaded chain necklace, about 10 inches
8mm (or any size of your choice) silver rings, 2
Jump rings, 4
Silver spring ring clasp, 1
Glue

1. Take a 2 ft cord and fold it in half to find the center. Attach it to the donut bead using a Lark's Head Knot (LHK). Repeat with 5 more 2 ft cords.

2. Separate cords 4-4-4. Tie a Square Knot (SK) with each set of 4 cords.

3. Move the left cord to the right as the Holding Cord (HC). Tie a Diagonal Double Half Hitch (DDHH) knot onto it with each of the next 5 cords, working from outside to inside.

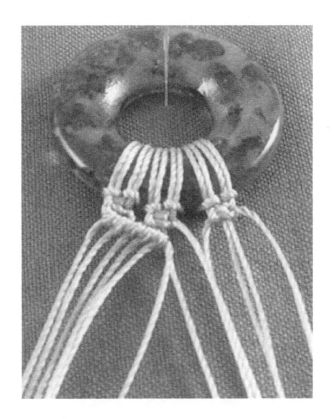

4. Move the right cord to the left as the HC. Tie a DDHH knot onto it with each of the next 5 cords, working from outside to inside.

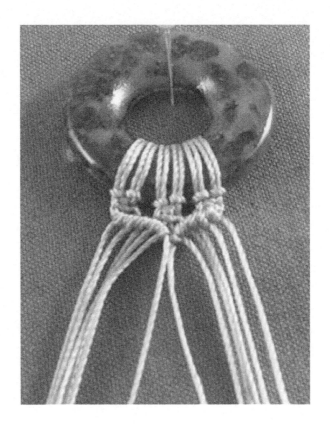

5. Place a 3mm raspberry bead onto the center 2 cords.

6. Working with the left cords, move the left cord to the right as the HC, then tie a DDHH knot onto it with each of the with next 3 cords, working from outside to inside.

7. Move the 3rd cord from the left to the left as the HC. Tie a DDHH knot onto it with next each of the next 2 cords, working from inside to outside.

8. Move the left cord to the right as the HC. Tie a DDHH knot onto it with each of the next 2 cords working from outside to inside.

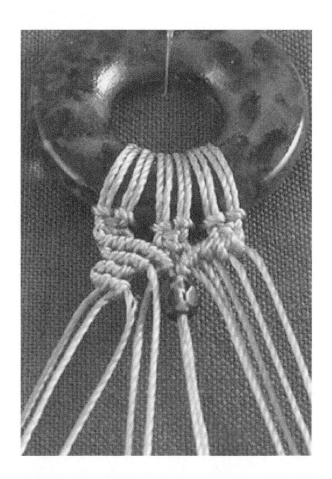

9. Move the left cord to the right as the HC. Tie a DDHH knot onto it with each of the next 3 cords, working from outside to inside.

10. Working with the right cords, move the right cord to the left as the HC, then tie a DDHH knot onto it with each of the with next 3 cords, working from outside to inside.

11.   Move the 3rd cord from the right to the right as the HC. Tie a DDHH knot onto it with next each of the next 2 cords, working from inside to outside.

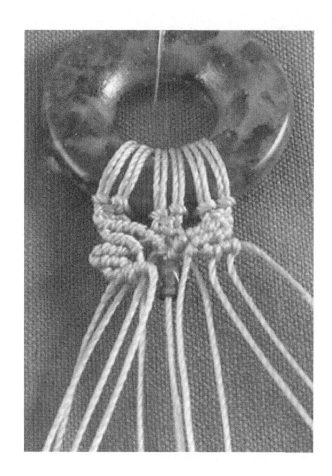

12. Move the right cord to the left as the HC. Tie a DDHH knot onto it with each of the next 2 cords working from outside to inside.

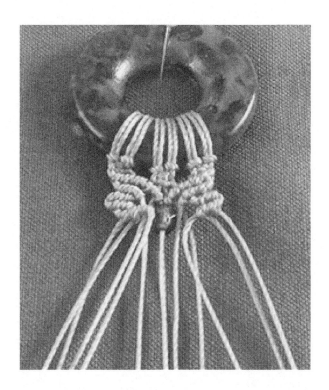

13. Move the right cord to the left as the HC. Tie a DDHH knot onto it with each of the next 3 cords, working from outside to inside.

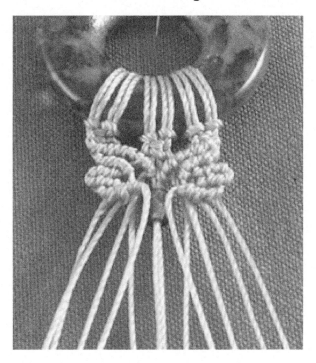

14. Move the center left cord to the left as the HC. Tie a DDHH knot onto it with each of the next 5 cords, working from inside to

outside.

15.   Move the center right cord to the right as the HC. Tie a DDHH knot onto it with each of the next 5 cords, working from inside to outside.

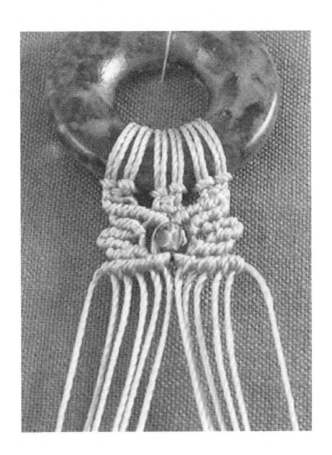

16. Working with the left cords, set aside the left cord. Place a size 10 pink seed bead onto the left cord. Move the 5th cord from the left to the left as the HC then tie a DDHH knot onto it with each of the next 4 cords, working from inside to outside.

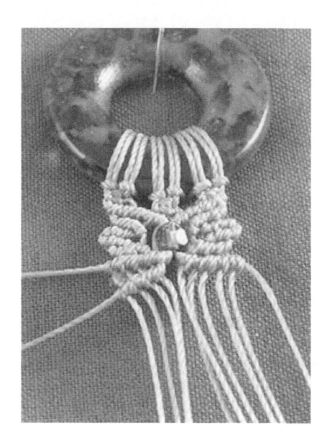

17. Working with the right cords, set aside the right cord. Place a size 10 pink seed bead onto the right cord. Move the 5th cord from the right to the right as the HC then tie a DDHH knot onto it with each of the next 4 cords, working from inside to outside.

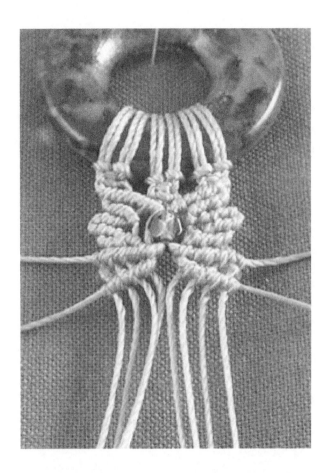

18.   Working with the left cords, set aside the left cord. Place a size 10 pink seed bead onto the left cord. Move the 4th cord from the left to the left as the HC then tie a DDHH knot onto it with each of the next 3 cords, working from inside to outside.

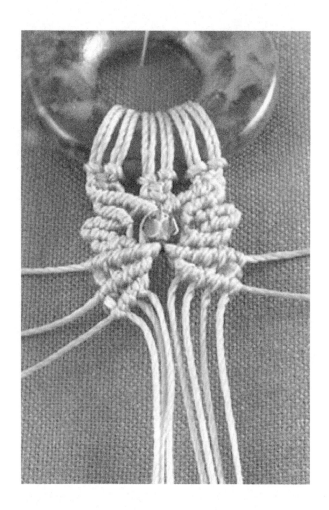

19. Working with the right cords, set aside the right cord. Place a size 10 pink seed bead onto the right cordMove the 4th cord from the right to the right as the HC then tie a DDHH knot onto it with each of the next 3 cords, working from inside to outside.

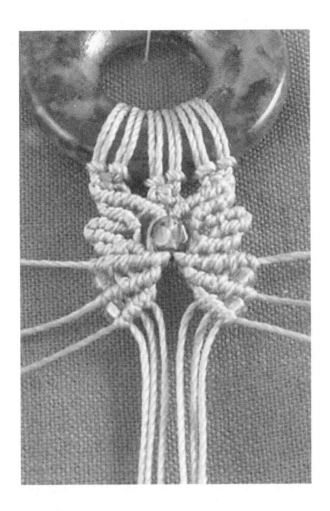

20. With the left 3 cords, move the 3rd cord from the left to the left as the HC. Tie a DDHH knot onto it with each of the next 2 cords, working from inside to outside.

21. With the right 3 cords, move the 3rd cord from the right to the right as the HC. Tie a DDHH knot onto it with each of the next 2 cords, working from inside to outside.

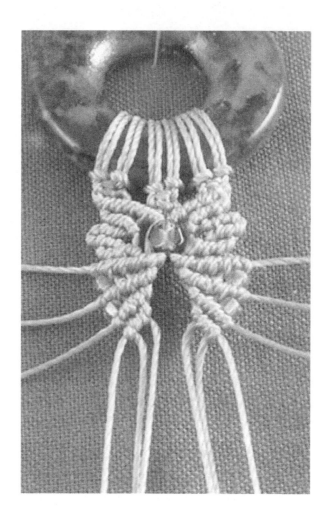

22. Move the 2nd cord from the left to the left as the HC. Tie a DDHH knot onto it with the next cord.

23. Move the 2nd cord from the right to the right as the HC. Tie a DDHH knot onto it with the next cord.

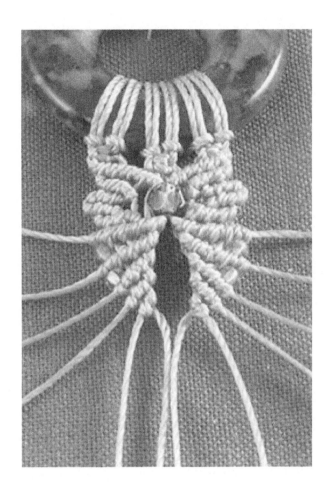

24. Working with the center 2 cords, move the right to the left as the HC. Tie a DDHH knot onto it with the left cord.

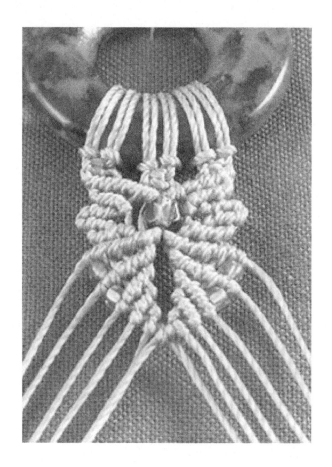

Upper section:
1. Take a 5ft cord and attach it to the donut bead (opposite of the previous work) using a LHK. Repeat with three more 5ft cords. Turn so the cords are facing down on your work surface.

2. Separate cords 4-4. Tie a SK with each set of 4 cords.

3. Move the 4th cord from the right to the left as the HC. Tie a DDHH knot onto it with each of the next 4 cords, working from right to left. (Keeping the HC tight against the previous knots as you go).

4. Move the 4th cord from the left to the left as the HC. Tie a DDHH knot onto it with each of the next 3 cords, working from right to left.

5. Move the 3rd cord from the left to the left as the HC. Tie a DDHH knot onto it with each of the next 2 cords, working from right to left.

6. Using the left cord as the HC, move it to the right and tie a DDHH knot onto it with each of the next 2 cords, working from left to right.

7. Move the left cord to the right as the HC. Tie a DDHH knot onto it with each of the next 3 cords, working from left to right.

8. Take the 4th cord in from the right and move it to the right as the HC. Tie a DDHH knot onto it with each of the next 3 cords, working from left to right.

9. Move the 3rd cord from the right to the right as the HC. Tie a DDHH knot onto it with each of the next 2 cords, working from left to right.

10. Move the right cord to the left as the HC. Tie a DDHH knot onto it with each of the next 2 cords, working from right to left.

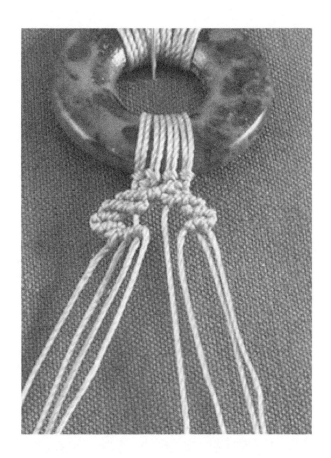

11. Move the right cord to the left as the HC. Tie a DDHH onto it with each of the next 3 cords, working from right to left.

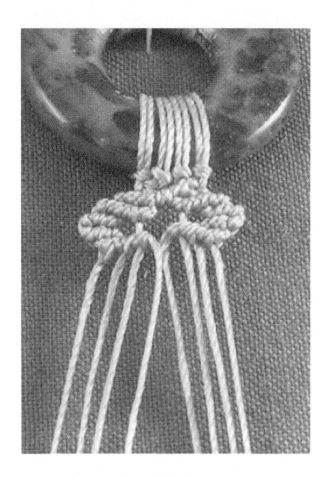

12. Place a 3mm raspberry bead onto the center 2 cords.

13. Use the left cord to tie a VLH knot around the 2 cords next to it. Repeat twice.

14. Use the right cord to tie a VLH knot around the 2 cords next to it. Repeat twice.

15. Place all cords together and tie a Square Knot (SK) with the outer cords.

16. Separate cords 4-4.

Working with the left 4 cords:
17. Move the 3rd cord from the left to the left as the HC. Tie a DDHH knot onto it with each of the next 2 cords, working from right to left.

18.   Move the 2nd cord from the right to the right as the HC. Tie a DDHH knot onto it with the right cord.

19.   Move the left cord to the right as the HC. Tie a DDHH knot onto it with the 2nd cord from the left.

20.   Move the right cord to the left as the HC. Tie a DDHH knot onto it with 2nd cord from the right.

21. Place the center right cord over the center left cord. Tie a DDHH knot with the left cord onto the right cord.

22. Move the 2nd cord from the left to the left as the HC. Tie a DDHH knot onto it with the left cord.

23. Repeat step 18-21.

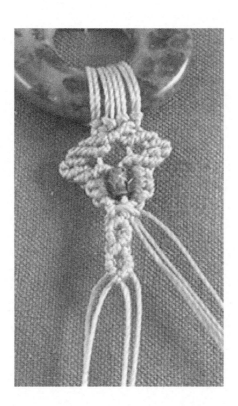

24.   Separate cords 2-2. With the left 2 cords, use the outer cord to tie 5 Vertical Lark's Head (VLH) knots onto the inner cord.

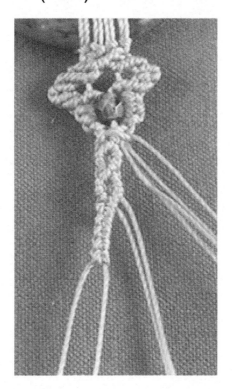

25. With the right 2 cords, use the outer cord to tie 5 (VLH) knots onto the inner cord.

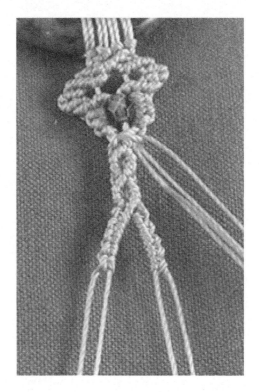

26. Repeat steps 17-23.

27. Thread a 4mm raspberry bead onto the center 2 cords.

1. Repeat steps 17-26.

Working with the right 4 cords:
29.   Repeat steps 17-28 with the right 4 cords.

Finishing:
Turn so that the loose cords are at the top of your work surface, then flip the necklace to the back side. Place the center 2 left cords through an 8mm silver ring then bring them straight down on top of the necklace. Tie a SK around the center cords (but not around the necklace) with the outer cords. Repeat with the right 4 cords. Glue the back of all last knots. Let dry, then trim excess cords. Attach your choice of chain (beaded or unbeaded) onto the 8mm rings, adding jump rings if necessary.

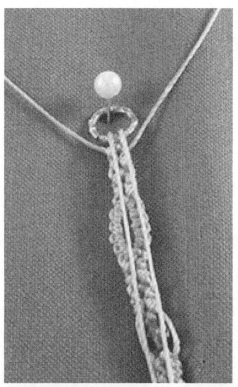

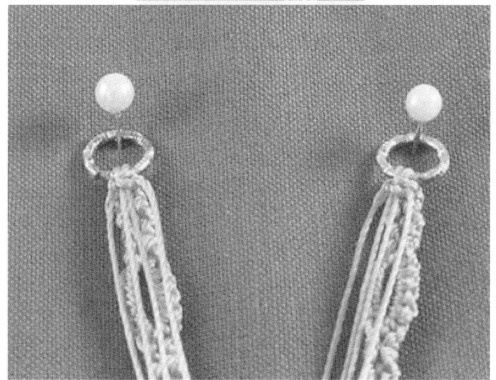

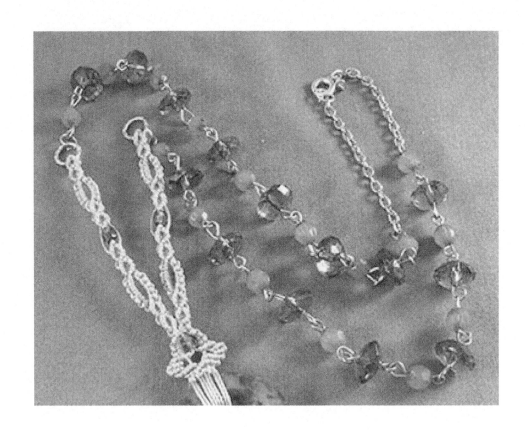

Eye of the Storm Pendant

Minimal beading allows the knotting to be the star of the show in this alluring pendant. A twist here, a double half hitch there and this stunning design is rapidly created. Add a charm and a chain of your choice to this 1 ½ inch piece.

Supplies:
Hyacinth C-Lon cord, 6 cords, 3 ½ ft each
5mm silver bead, 1
3mm silver bead (or a size 6 silver seed bead) 1
Size 11 silver seed beads, 8
1cm silver charm, 1
Chain of your choice
Glue

1. Hold all 6 cords together and tie a loose overhand knot in the center. Pin onto your work surface as shown.

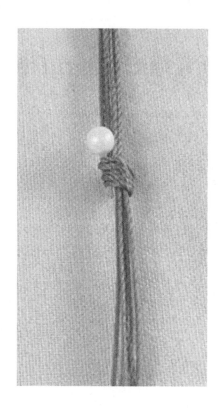

2. Tie 7 Square Knots (SK) with the outer 2 cords around all others.

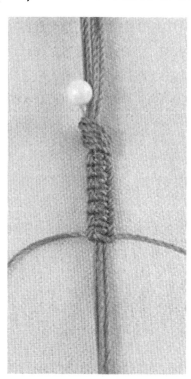

3. Untie the overhand knot then fold the SK section in half. Tie another SK using the outer cords from the bottom section.

4. Find the 3rd cord in from the left and move it to the left as the Holding Cord (HC). Tie a Diagonal Double Half Hitch (DDHH) knot onto it with the 2nd cord from the left, then with the 1st cord on the left.

5. Find the 3rd cord in from the right and move it to the right as the HC. Tie a DDHH knot onto it with the 2nd cord from the right, then with the 1st cord on the right.

6. Move the left cord to the right and tie a DDHH knot onto it with the next 4 cords, working from outside to inside.

7. Move the right cord to the left and tie a DDHH knot onto it with the next 4 cords, working from outside to inside.

8. Place a 5mm silver bead onto the center 2 cords. Move the left HC to the right and tie a DDHH knot onto it with the left center cord. Move the right HC to the left and tie a DDHH knot onto it with the right center cord.

9. Move the right HC to the left and tie a DDHH knot onto it with the left HC, to close the diamond shape.

10. Place a size 11 seed bead onto the 2nd and 4th cords in from each side.

11. Place the left cord down and in toward the center as the HC. Tie a DDHH knot onto it with each of the next 5 cords, working from outside to inside.

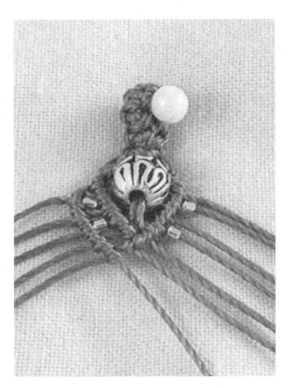

12. Place the right cord down and in toward the center as the HC. Tie a DDHH knot onto it with each of the next 5 cords, working from outside to inside.

13.   Move the center right cord over the center left cord. Tie a DDHH knot onto the right cord with the left.

14. Separate cords 2-2-4-2-2. Starting with the left 2 cords, use the outer cord to tie about 2cm worth of Half Hitch (HH) knots (about 25 knots) onto the inner cord, creating a spiral.

15. Repeat with each set of 2 cords, using the outer cord to tie onto the inner cord each time.

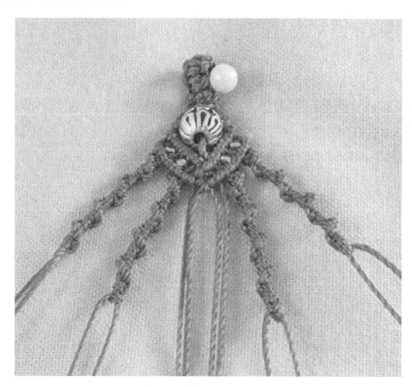

16.   Move the 6th cord from the left to the left as the HC. Tie a DDHH knot onto it with the 5th cord from the left.

17.   Move the 6th cord from the right to the right as the HC. Tie a DDHH knot onto it with the 5th cord from the right.

18.   Place a 3mm silver bead (or a size 6 seed bead) onto the center 2 cords. Take the 5th cord from the left and move it to the right as the HC, then tie a DDHH knot onto it with the 6th cord from the left. Move the 5th cord from the right to the left as the HC, then tie a DDHH knot onto it with the 6th cord from the right. Using the center 2 cords place the right cord over the left and tie a DDHH knot with left cord onto the right cord.

19. Take the left spiral cord and place it in toward the center, over top of the inner left spiral cord. Use one cord from this spiral as the HC and place it in to the right. Tie a DDHH knot onto it with each of the next 3 cords, working from left to right.

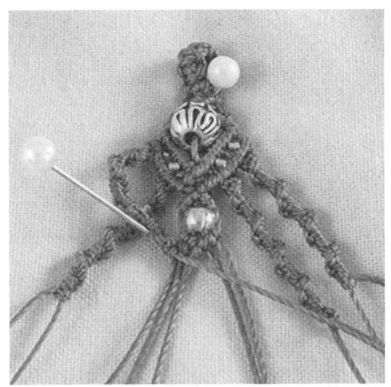

20. Take the outer right spiral cord and place it in toward the center, over top of the inner right spiral cord. Use one cord from this spiral

as the HC and place it in to the left. Tie a DDHH knot onto it with each of the next 3 cords, working from right to left.

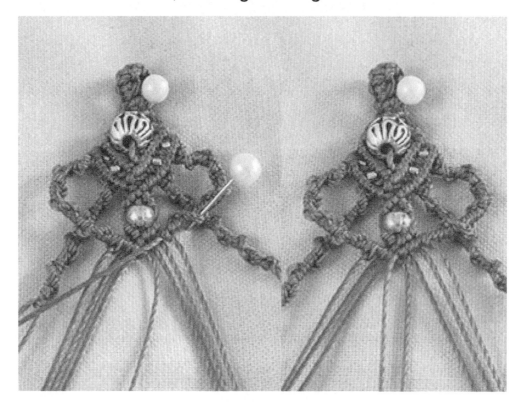

21.   Working with the center 2 cords, move the right over the left and tie a DDHH knot with the left cord onto the right cord.

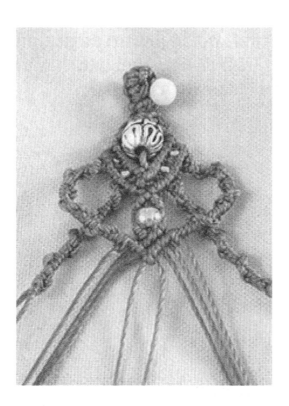

22.   Place a seed bead onto the 3rd and 5th cords in from each side.

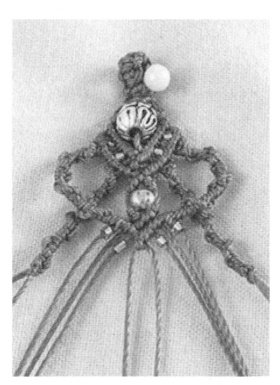

23.   Move the left spiral knot in toward center, and place one cord to the right as the HC. Tie a DDHH knot onto it with each of the next 5 cords, working from outside to inside.

24.   Move the right spiral knot in toward center, and place one cord to the left as the HC. Tie a DDHH knot onto it with each of the next 5 cords, working from outside to inside.

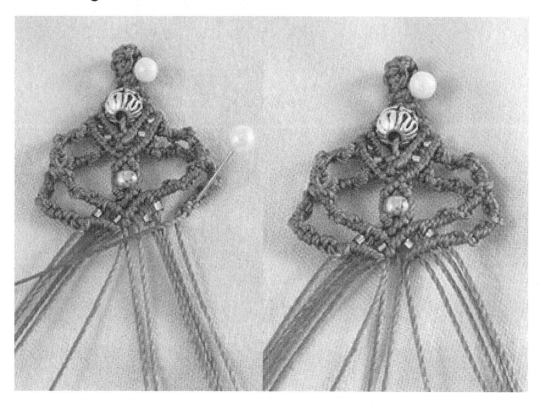

25.   Repeat step 21.

26.   Set aside the outer cord on each side. Place the left cord down and in toward the center as the HC. Tie a DDHH knot onto it with each of the next 4 cords, working from outside to inside. Place the right cord down and in toward the center as the HC. Tie a DDHH knot onto it with each of the next 4 cords, working from outside to inside. Move the center right over the center left cord then tie a DDHH knot with the left cord onto the right.

27. Set aside the outer cord on each side. Place the left cord down and in toward the center as the HC. Tie a DDHH knot onto it with each of the next 3 cords, working from outside to inside. Place the right cord down and in toward the center as the HC. Tie a DDHH knot onto it with each of the next 3 cords, working from outside to inside. Move the center right over the center left cord then tie a DDHH knot with the left cord onto the right.

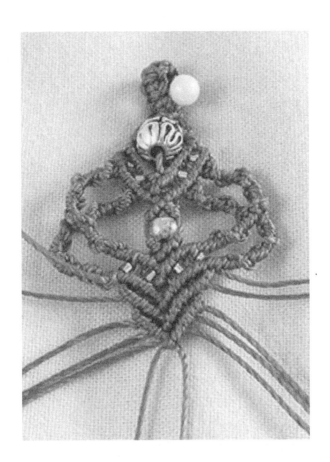

28.   Take the silver charm and thread the center 2 cords through it from front to back.

29. Turn the pendant over so the back side is facing up. Now rotate until that the center 2 cords are at the top of your board. Bring the center 2 cords down toward you, laying them on top of the pendant.

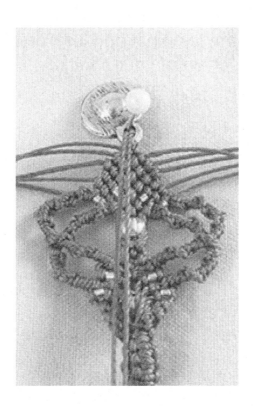

Use the cord on the left and the cord on the right to tie a square knot around the center cords.

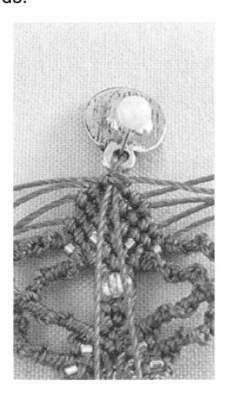

Place a bit of glue on the last knot and let it dry. Trim excess cords.
Place pendant onto a chain of your choice.

Wildwood Necklace

This striking necklace gives you the chance to learn and practice the Margaretenspitze (Margarete Lace) style of knotting. It is one of only a very few patterns of this method available in English. Half hitch and double half hitch knots are used extensively in this 11.5 inch length necklace. A multi-colored silk ribbon and a toggle clasp complete this piece.

Supplies:
Fern C-Lon cord , 4 cords, 5ft 4in each
8mm antique gold ring, 2
Size 8 purple seed beads, 6
Size 11 purple seed beads, 7
7mm purple bead, 1

Silk ribbon about 2-4ft, depending on your closure choice (see Note)
Antique gold toggle clasp closure set, 1
Glue
Ribbon crimps, 2 (optional) *Note: there are 2 closure options written into this pattern. If you choose the overhand knot (pictured) then you will not need the ribbon crimps, and will use less ribbon.*

1. Attach a Fern C-Lon cord to an 8mm antique gold ring using a Lark's Head Knot (LHK). Repeat with the 3 remaining cords.

2. Tie a Square Knot (SK) with the 4 left cords.

3. Move the right cord to the left as the Holding Cord (HC), then tie a Diagonal Double Half Hitch (DDHH) knot onto it with each of the next 7 cords, working from right to left.

4. Working with the right 4 cords, move the 2nd cord from the right to the left as the HC. Tie a DDHH knot onto it with each of the next 2 cords, working from right to left.

5. Move the 2nd cord from the right to the right as the HC. Tie a DDHH knot onto it with the right cord.

6. Place the 2nd and 3rd cord from the right together and thread on a size 8 purple seed bead.

7. Move the 4th cord from the right to the right as the HC. Tie a DDHH knot onto it with the 3rd cord from the right.

8. Move the right cord to the left as the HC and tie a DDHH knot onto it with the 2nd cord from the right.

9. Move the 2nd cord from the right to the left as the HC. Tie a DDHH knot onto it with the 3rd cord from the right.

10.   Move the 3rd cord from the right to the left as the HC. Tie a DDHH knot onto it with the 4th cord from the right.

11. Repeat step 5-10.

12. Repeat steps 5-9.

13. Working with the left 4 cords, use the left cord to tie 20 Half Hitch (HH) knots around the other three cords.

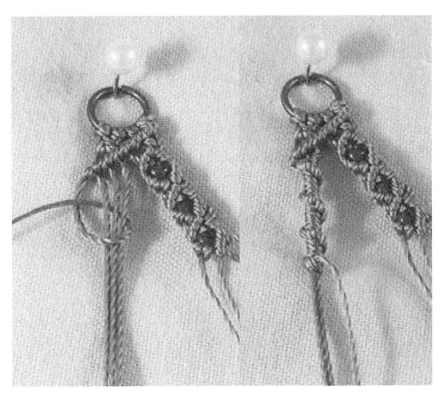

14. Set aside the 2 left cords, then move the 3rd cord from the left to the right as the HC. Tie a DDHH knot onto it with each of the next 2 cords, working from left to right.

15. Take the right cord and move it to the left as the HC. Tie a DDHH knot onto it with each of the next 3 cords, working from right to left.

16. Place a size 11 purple seed bead onto the right cord. Move it to the left as the HC. Tie a DDHH knot onto it with each of the next 3 cords, working from right to left.

17.   Repeat step 16 twice.

Working with the 4 left cords:
18.   Move the 3rd cord from the left to the left as HC, then tie a DDHH knot onto it with each of the next 2 cords, working from right to left.

19. Move the 3rd cord from the left to the right as the HC, tie a DDHH knot onto it with the 4th cord in from the left.

20.   Place the 2nd cord and the 3rd cord from the left together and thread on a size 8 purple seed bead.

21.   Move the left cord to the right as the HC. Tie a DDHH knot onto it with the 2nd cord from the left.

22.   Move the 4th cord from the left to the left as the HC, tie a DDHH knot onto it with the 3rd cord from the left.

23. Move the 3rd cord from the left to the left as the HC, tie a DDHH knot onto it with the 2nd cord from the left.

Working with all cords:

24. Move the 4th cord from the right to the left as the HC. Tie a DDHH knot onto it with each of the next 4 cords, working from right to left.

25. Set aside the right cord. Place the next right cord to the left as the HC and tie a DDHH knot onto it with each of the next 6 cords, working from right to left.

26. Set aside the right cord. Place the next right cord to the left as the HC and tie a DDHH knot onto it with each of the next 5 cords, working from right to left.

27. Set aside the right cord. Place the next right cord to the left as the HC and tie a DDHH knot onto it with each of the next 4 cords, working from right to left.

28. Set aside the right cord. Place the next right cord to the left as the HC and tie a DDHH knot onto it with each of the next 3 cords, working from right to left.

29.   Move the left cord to the right as the HC then tie a DDHH knot onto it with each of the next 3 cords, working from left to right.

30.   Move the left cord to the right as the HC then tie a DDHH knot onto it with each of the next 4 cords, working from left to right.

31. Move the left cord to the right as the HC then tie a DDHH knot onto it with each of the next 5 cords, working from left to right.

32. Move the left cord to the right as the HC then tie a DDHH knot onto it with each of the next 6 cords, working from left to right.

33. Move the left cord to the right as the HC then tie a DDHH knot onto it with each of the next 7 cords, working from left to right.

34.   Set aside the 3 right cords. Move the next right cord to the left
as the HC, then tie a DDHH knot onto it with each of the next 4 cords,
working from right to left.

35. Set aside the right cord. Move the next right cord to the left as the HC, then tie a DDHH knot onto it with each of the next 3 cords, working from right to left.

36. Set aside the right cord. Move the next right cord to the left as HC, then tie a DDHH knot onto it with each of the next 2 cords, working from right to left.

37. Set aside the right cord. Move the next right cord to the left as the HC, then tie a DDHH knot onto it with the next cord.

38.   Move the left cord to the right as the HC. Tie a DDHH knot onto it with the next cord.

39.   Move the left cord to the right as the HC. Tie a DDHH knot onto the HC with each of the next 2 cords, working from left to right.

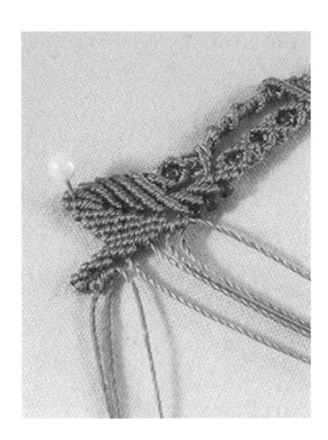

40. Move the left cord to the right as the HC. Tie a DDHH knot onto the HC with each of the next 3 cords, working from left to right.

41. Move the left cord to the right as the HC. Tie a DDHH knot onto the HC with each of the next 4 cords, working from left to right.

42. Separate cords 4-4. With the 4 right cords, take the right cord and tie 18 HH knots around the other 3 cords.

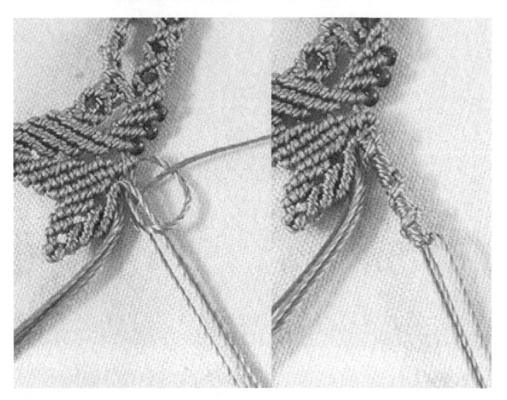

43. Working with the left 4 cords, tie a SK with the 3 right cords. Place a size 11 seed bead onto the left cord then move to the right as the HC. Tie a DDHH knot onto it with each of the next 3 cords, working from left to right. Repeat the bead and the DDHH knots 3 times.

44.   Place the bundled right cords over top of the left cords. Tie a
DDHH knot around the bundle, with each of the left cords, working
from right to left.

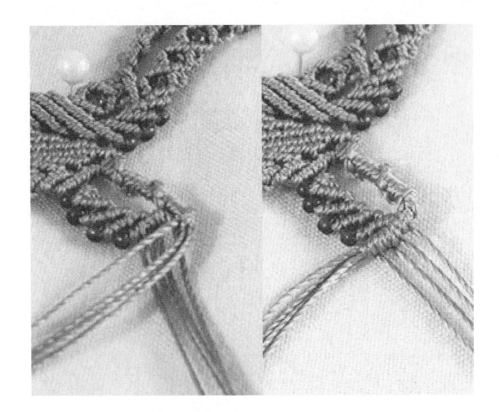

45. Use the left cord to tie 6 Vertical Lark's Head (VLH) knots around the 2nd cord in from the left. Place a size 8 purple seed bead onto the left cord. Place a 7mm purple bead onto the 3rd and 4th cords from the left. Tie 5 VLH knots with the left cord onto a bundle made of cords 2, 3 and 4 from the left, then move this cord bundle up to the right.

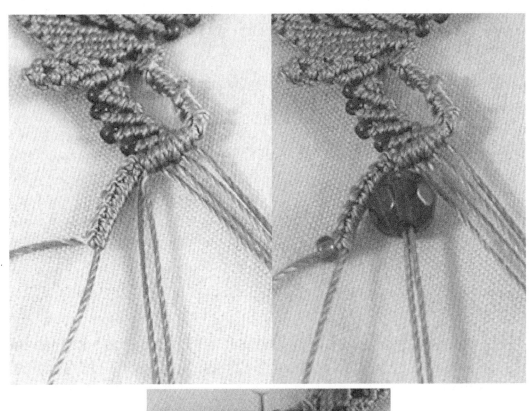

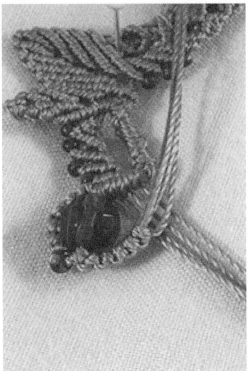

46. Tie a DDHH knot around the cord bundle with each of the next 4 cords, working from left to right.

293

47.   Separate cords 3-2-3. With the left set of 3 cords use the left cord to tie HH knots onto the other 2 cords for a length of 3cm (about 40 HH knots).

48.   With the center 2 cords, use the left cord to tie HH knots onto the right cord for a length of 2 ½ cm (about 31 HH knots).

49.   With the right 3 cords use the right cord to tie HH knots onto the other 2 cords for a length of 2cm (about 25 HH knots).

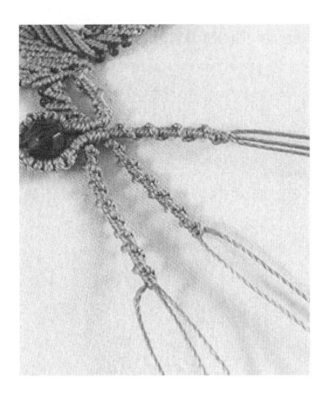

50.   Take the right set of spiral cords and lay them together with the center spiral HC. Use the Wrapping Cord (WC) from the center bundle to tie a DHH knot around all 4 HC.

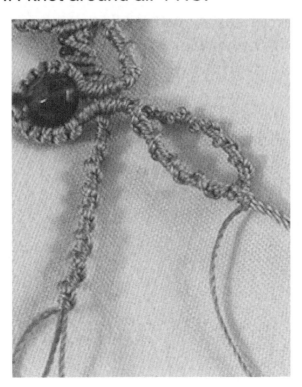

51. Move the left spiral through the opening just created.

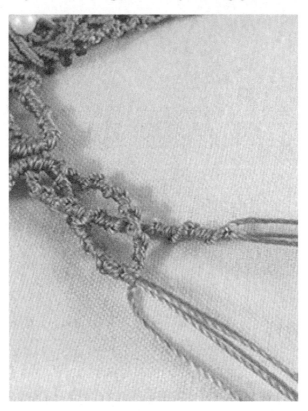

52. Find the (new) left spiral and tie HH knots with the left cord around the rest of the bundle for ½ cm (about 5 HH knots).

53.   Move the left cord to the right as the HC. Tie a DDHH knot onto it with each of the next 7 cords, working from left to right.

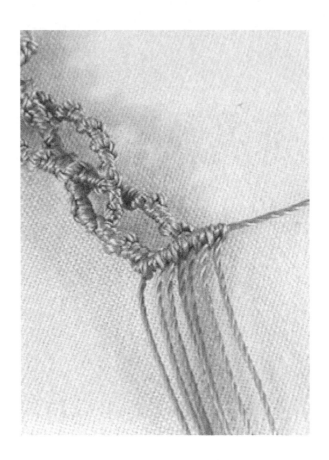

54. Set aside the left cord. Place the new left cord to the right and tie a DDHH knot onto it with each of the next 6 cords, working from left to right.

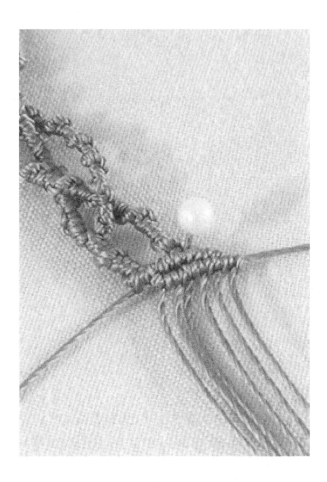

55. Set aside the left cord. Place the new left cord to the right and tie a DDHH knot onto it with each of the next 5 cords, working from left to right.

56. Set aside the left cord. Place the new left cord to the right and tie a DDHH knot onto it with each of the next 4 cords, working from left to right.

57. Set aside the left cord. Place the new left cord to the right and tie a DDHH knot onto it with each of the next 3 cords, working from left to right.

58. Place a size 8 seed bead onto the right cord then thread this cord through an 8mm antique gold ring and back through the size 8 seed bead.

59. Place the right cord to the left and tie a DDHH knot onto it with each of the next 3 cords, working from right to left.

60. Place the right cord to the left and tie a DDHH knot onto it with each of the next 4 cords, working from right to left.

61. Place the right cord to the left and tie a DDHH knot onto it with each of the next 5 cords, working from right to left.

62. Place the right cord to the left and tie a DDHH knot onto it with each of the next 6 cords, working from right to left.

63. Place the right cord to the left and tie a DDHH knot onto it with each of the next 7 cords, working from right to left.

64. Set aside the 3 left cords. Move the new left cord to the right as the HC. Tie a DDHH knot onto it with each of the next 4 cords, working from left to right.

65. Set aside the left cord.   Move the new left cord to the right as the HC. Tie a DDHH knot onto it with each of the next 3 cords, working from left to right.

66. Set aside the left cord. Move the new left cord to the right as the HC. Tie a DDHH knot onto it with each of the next 2 cords, working from left to right.

67. Set aside the left cord. Move the new left cord to the right as the HC. Tie a DDHH knot onto it with the next cord.

68.   Move the right cord to the left as the HC. Tie a DDHH knot onto it with the first cord, working from right to left.

69. Move the right cord to the left as the HC. Tie a DDHH knot onto it with each of the next 2 cords, working from right to left.

70. Move the right cord to the left as the HC. Tie a DDHH knot onto it with each of the next 3 cords, working from right to left.

71. Move the right cord to the left as the HC. Tie a DDHH knot onto it with each of the next 4 cords, working from right to left.

72.   Glue the back side of each ending knot, let dry, then trim all excess cords OR trim excess cords leaving a little stump, then singe the ends with a singe tool. Place a bit of glue on the back side of each final knot.

73. Two ribbon closure options are available to you: knotting,or using ribbon clasp crimps. The knotted version works best if your cord is pliable, or more like fabric. I am using silk ribbon.

<u>Clasp option</u>: Thread about 2ft of ribbon through each 8mm ring and center it. Paint the end(s) of the ribbon with glue and place in the crimp end. Crimp shut. Attach jump rings (if necessary) and a toggle (or spring ring and jump ring) closure.

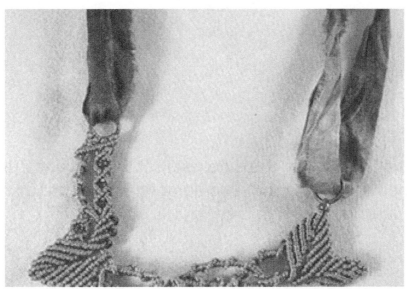

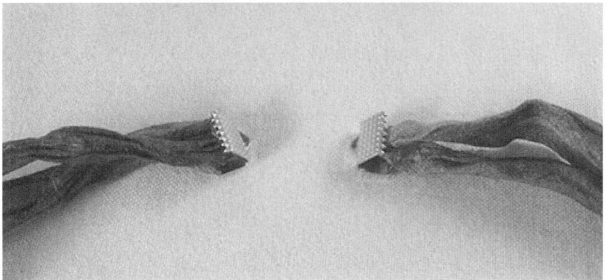

<u>Knotted option</u>: Place ribbon through the 8mm antique gold ring from front to back (determine the length of ribbon you want because you will have more ribbon to work with since we are not doubling it up).

Tuck the short end of the ribbon inside the long piece.

Tie an overhand knot with the side nearest the necklace (the 8mm ring) first, then set your length and tie another overhand knot near the toggle closure end.

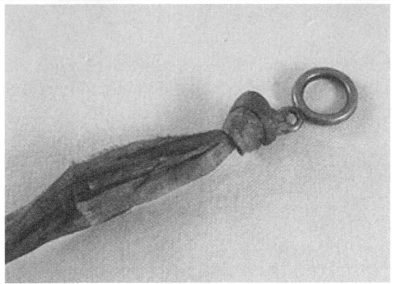

Once you are happy with the placement of all your knots, separate the short end of the ribbon and place a bit of glue the inside of the knot. Trim the SHORT end of the ribbon. Glue again if desired or if your cords fray a lot (like mine). Feel free to add a jump ring to the toggle clasp and thread the ribbon through that if necessary.

I went with the knotted closure for a couple of reasons; I could only find the crimp clasps in silver, which didn't match my other metals, and I felt the knots would compliment the casual look of the ribbon I was using.

The end
Thank you!

Printed in Great Britain
by Amazon

44557377R00172